1982

SPEAKING
to Inform
and Persuade

SPEAKING
to Inform
and Persuade

SECOND EDITION

Otis M. Walter

Professor of Rhetorical Theory
University of Pittsburgh

MACMILLAN PUBLISHING CO., INC.
New York

COLLIER MACMILLAN PUBLISHERS
London

Macmillan Publishing Co., Inc.
866 Third Avenue, New York, New York 10022

Collier Macmillan Canada, Ltd.

Library of Congress Cataloging in Publication Data

Walter, Otis M
    Speaking to inform and persuade.

    Bibliography: p.
    Includes index.
    1. Public speaking.   I. Title.
PN4121.W324   1982   808.5'1   80-29640
ISBN 0-02-424400-7

Contents

6 Persuasive Logic: The Tactics of Persuasion 51

7 Emotion and Motivation: The Strategy of Persuasion 85

8 The Ethos of the Speaker 109

9 Delivery 137

10 Assignments in Exposition and Persuasion 147

1
Speaking to Inform and Persuade

WHAT PEOPLE SAY to each other can change what happens in the world. What happens in our world depends in part on whether speakers put people to sleep or wake them up. But what happens depends on much more: on whether speakers speak intelligently or stupidly, rationally or irrationally, powerfully or weakly, ethically or unethically, persuasively or ineffectively. Speaking is one of the links in the chain of causes that pull civilizations either up or down or that bind civilizations to a stultifying changelessness.

Societies have paid a high price and continue to suffer from the effects of allowing themselves to be mislead by blind, ineffective and selfish orators. Speakers have influenced societies to fight wars, persecute the innocent, the innovative, the weak or the different. They have swayed populations to allow tyranny or permit poverty to be ignored and increased. Consequently, civilizations have crumbled and died. All cultures have had their share of such speakers. Who are the speakers today who mislead? Certainly, if we asked ten people to name

1

them, we would not find much agreement, but we would probably find no one who would say "No speaker misleads, today; misleading died with . . . . (the Middle Ages, 1776, World War II, or the election of . . .)." Even if our own culture has had its share of such speakers, we have escaped, so far, the ultimate fate of unwise speaking, but muddled, malicious and personally ambitious speakers have taken a toll.

Although speaking can harm, it can also help. It can unleash our sources of energy, crystalize our vague conceptions, enable us to understand and partly control our destiny, and lead us intelligently. We might all agree that the speaking in support of the Declaration of Independence helped the colonists recognize that people had self-evident rights to life, liberty, and the pursuit of happiness, and that government was instituted not to rule but to secure those rights. Speaking today may make us forget that the aim of government, according to the Declaration, was to secure rights for us. But the point is that speaking can help direct us wisely and powerfully, just as it can fall far short of our needs. Among our greatest needs is to produce speakers who can identify our shortcomings and show us that we can and, must overcome them.

Courses in speech, when taught in certain ways, can help develop speakers who are a credit to our civilization and a help to us. Naturally no speech course alone is sufficient to produce the kind of speakers we need, but the right kind of course can help produce individuals who are clear instead of muddled, interesting, instead of dull, thoughtful instead of superficial, and powerful instead of weak. Moreover, such courses can indirectly produce such speakers by helping to develop intelligent *listeners*—listeners who demand speakers who help us discern our complicated difficulties, who clarify rather than obscure, and who take reason as far as reason can go. Sophisticated listeners will not tolerate uninformed, irrationally prejudiced, or morally bankrupt speakers. When we have enough sophisticated listeners to understand, appreciate, and demand quality in speaking, we are more apt to have better speakers.

This book, *Speaking to Inform and Persuade*, is an attempt to present the fundamentals of clear, intelligent, and vivid speaking. It is an attempt to provide the tools without which there cannot be the kind of speaking that helps us understand and control our future. The tools exist, and to explain them and make them useful, we must explore many subjects. We will need to look into some areas of modern psychology, into aspects of human reasoning, into notions of ethics, and, of course, into rhetoric. In this brief book, one cannot explore all the means by which human beings lead others to understanding; but *the aim of this book is to provide some crucial essentials that enable one's speeches to be of service to one's fellow human beings.*

Although this book is entitled *Speaking to Inform and Persuade*, there is no utility in drawing a sharp line between the processes of exposition and those of persuasion. These processes, although perhaps distinguishable, are inseparable: good exposition often will change beliefs and attitudes—that is, it will persuade—and good persuasion often will present information. Yet at an early stage in educating speakers, the distinction is useful, so let us use it temporarily. By *informative speaking* we mean speaking appropriate to situations in which the audience is not hostile to the speaker's ideas and in which the speaker needs only to present those ideas with maximum clarity and vividness. By *persuasion* we mean a more difficult task: Persuasive speaking is appropriate to situations in which the speaker wishes to change or heighten the attitudes, beliefs, values, or behavior of an audience. We will take up the simpler tasks first—those of achieving clarity and vividness; they will form the basis for the more difficult tasks of persuasion.

Exercises

1. Give examples of speakers who helped their society understand its problems. Explain why you believe they helped.

2. Give examples of speakers who prevented people from understanding their problems. Explain why you selected them.

3. If we need speakers who can help us recognize and solve problems, which problems are most pressing?

4. List some trivial problems that seem to concern some people, but that you believe are relatively unimportant.

5. Give a two-minute impromptu speech on "The most important problem I know" or "An important problem that is often overlooked."

6. Give a five-minute speech on "How problems caused the downfall of the civilization of Greece, Rome, Egypt, or any culture or country of your choice."

7. If speakers mislead, why do they? Choose three speakers who you think have misled people and explain why you think they did. Why is it difficult to be sure about why a speaker misleads?

8. Name a speaker you believe generally leads wisely. Explain why you think so. Would other people who also know the speaker agree with you? Why?

2
Exposition:
An Overview

The Significance of Exposition

Changing Perceptions
Dull informative speeches and memos may not change much of anything, but clear and vivid exposition may help people change direction. For example, we are apt to believe that speeding is the major cause of automobile accidents until we learn that most accidents occur at speeds below thirty-five miles an hour. Moreover, when we learn that at least one state, Connecticut, found that strict enforcement of speeding laws increased accidents, we are apt to wonder if speeding does cause accidents. Perhaps faster driving, within limits, reduces accidents because driving fast is less frustrating than driving slowly, and because driving fast forces drivers to occupy themselves more fully with the task of driving. The information might make us give up the old idea that the enemy of safe driving is speed. But, the information is spotty: Now, that we have a national speed limit of fifty-five miles per hour, there are fewer accidents per

5

year. Nevertheless, perhaps there are fewer accidents because fewer people are driving fewer miles because of the increased price of gasoline—not to mention the increased price of automobiles—and the increased time that long trips take. We do not know. But if we did, we would have information that might change—or uphold—the idea that driving slowly might slightly reduce the number of accidents. What we do depends partly on the information we have.

With misinformation, we can be led into serious mistakes in both thought and behavior. Misinformation bolstered the belief in witches led to thousands of persecutions. When we believed that mentally ill people could be cured by torture, we used on unfortunate victims terrors that should shame a rational human being. Savage cults, acting on what they thought was information, sacrificed human beings to increase the yield of crops, or to secure a safe sea voyage, or to win at war. And with misinformation, the United States embarked on a war in Vietnam against guerillas that could not be won by standard armies, in support of one of Vietnam's two dictatorships, and lost. But with better information, societies might have changed. We need adequate information if society is to improve itself—indeed if it is to survive. Our own survival demands the best information we can get.

The Information Explosion

Information has taken on increased importance in our time, because our culture is experiencing an "information explosion." Just as population is rising explosively, and just as the amount of explosive power available is rising in somewhat the same way, so are amounts of information increasing with unprecedented speed. Information is increasing more rapidly than population or power. The amount of scientific information published each *day* could fill *eight sets* of the twenty-four volume *Encyclopaedia Britannica*. To read all the scientific material published in only a single day would take the average person, reading eight hours a day, about fourteen years. And after reading for fourteen years, only a single day's scientific writings would have been read. The reader would know little of that same day's other current events—and would know little of discoveries in philosophy or developments in foreign affairs, little of the arts and literature of the time, of the changes in religion, in government, or in industry. Despite fourteen years of reading, the reader would have an unbelievably narrow range of information.

The information available in the world *doubles approximately every eight years.* If this enormous growth of information is to have a desirable influence, it must, somehow, be digested, comprehended, and communicated. Because information can change society and because the amount of information doubles every eight years, our culture, if it is to become enriched and improved by its information, needs speakers and writers to digest and assimilate information and to present it to us with clarity. The development of intelligent, informative speakers is necessary for the improvement of our society.

A New Art Form

Another reason informative discourse is significant is more speculative and less certain: Informative discourse, including not only speeches but written matter, is becoming a new art form. Each great age has had its memorable art forms: the Greeks had the dialogue and the temple, the Elizabethans had the drama of Shakespeare, the romantics had their poets, and the nineteenth century had great novelists. Some say—although not all believe it—that our age is not distinguished for its drama, for although we perform many plays, we have not produced playwrights the equal of Sophocles or Shakespeare; others say that our poets seem to write only for each other, that our architecture has become the servant of business efficiency, and our art hardly equals the greatness of Leonardo's; that to listen to modern "serious" music is an irritating chore. But informative discourse—especially as presented in the superior college lecture or the occasionally superior article in one of the better magazines—is a form that can keep a whole people abreast of our bursting development. Superior informative discourse is compact, beautiful, intelligent, and sometimes, as in the hands of a Bertrand Russell, a Loren Eisley, a Rachel Carson, or a Barbara Tuchman, inspiring. Never before has there been so much good exposition. And this form is uniquely suited to some of the needs of our time: we need to be kept informed as no people ever before. We need information not merely to stay "ahead," but to find new solutions to old problems, to find which problems have evaporated and which are just beginning to darken our horizon. We need to be kept informed, especially, if we are to make education and democratic government work. *If a civilization develops an art form in response to a need, the need for such an art form is there.* Never before have so many needed so much information about so many things. If we fail to select, digest, and assimilate the information of this age, the possibilities open to us will be severely limited. But there are signs that we are not failing: More people are reading information than ever before. Last year more people bought books than ever before, and in recent years nonfiction has been outselling fiction. Our magazines have reached all-time highs in circulation, and they abound in informative discourse that is sometimes subtle without being obscure, powerful without being bombastic, clear without being obtuse, beautiful without being arty, and profound without pomposity. We may, in expository discourse, have a new art form uniquely suited to the needs of our time.

On the Rewards for Good Speaking

Expository speaking is important to society; when we speak well, we perform a service to society. It is to be hoped that the fine speaker finds other rewards for service, even though there is no guarantee of reward. Generally, fine speaking does pay the rewards of satisfaction and of recognition from others. But those who are willing to serve their fellow human beings will find, sometimes, that to serve is its own reward. Galileo was put under house arrest for good exposition; Pasteur, for the same kind of crime, was ignored and lampooned by the medical profession; and Linus Pauling is derided because he writes and speaks in defense of vitamin C as a preventative for the common cold. Yet those who want to serve will not hesitate to do so, and if service must be its own reward, it will be sufficient. But we must recognize that when service is its own reward, we have a tragic situation, and a dangerous one.

Those more interested in personal success than in public service should not lightly pass the study of exposition by, and the reason is plain: If one attains any sort of prominence, one will be involved in communicating. If one is unable to communicate effectively, one risks the possibility of obscurity. To anyone who wishes prominence, it may be worth the time to look closely at the means by which information can be communicated intelligently.

The Basic Units of Discourse

The inner dynamics of our personality determine how we see the task of speaking. To one kind of person, giving a speech may seem a simple matter: "Have a few nice things to say and say them well." To a different kind of person, the task may appear so hopelessly difficult that it can never be learned well. Both notions are wrong.

Good speaking is difficult to develop, even in one of its simplest form, which is exposition. However, it is not so difficult that it cannot be learned by anyone who is intelligent and hard working. *It is possible to learn the skills of exposition and persuasion, difficult though they are, because discourses, whether expository or persuasive, are built out of certain simple units.* Just as a brick wall is built of simple units—bricks and mortar—so are speeches built of basic units. If you learn how to apply mortar to bricks and master a few other procedures, such as how to put in a foundation, you can build a sound wall. You also can learn to write and speak well by understanding how to use the basic units of discourse. These basic units are relatively few in number —although they are more complex than the basic units of a wall—but if they are not understood, your speeches may be much like walls built by a person who did not know the simple technique of building a straight wall by using a chalk line and a plumb line. Let us, therefore, turn to the basic units of all informative and persuasive discourse.

The study of exposition and persuasion is largely the study of the question "How do you gain acceptance for an idea?" The question means "How can you make an idea clear, interesting, palatable, vivid, logical, convincing, and persuasive?" Good speaking always involves two tasks, which together form the basic unit of expository and persuasive discourse: (1) identify as precisely as possible the *ideas* you want the audience to understand; (2) discover *support* for your ideas that will make them clear, interesting, and believable.

This division of the basic unit into ideas and their support may seem so obvious that its utility is lost on the beginner, and it will probably not reassure the novice to hear that this division is so useful it was recognized more than two thousand years ago by Aristotle and has been used in rhetoric ever since. From this division, however, spring countless techniques of varying degrees of intricacy; and the rest of this book is based on this division. As we study these divisions, you will see that they are indispensable.

The division of the basic unit into ideas and support is indeed, indispensable because it is as impossible to talk about building a speech without mentioning ideas and supporting material as it would be to talk about building a brick wall without mentioning bricks and mortar. Without mentioning ideas and support, we cannot discuss speeches intelligently; with them, we can give directions so that most readers can give a reasonably good speech without a hopelessly arduous expenditure of time and effort. Let us look at the characteristics of each of these materials.

Differentiating Between Ideas and Support

Ideas and their support are much like the differences between military strategy and tactics. Ideas, like strategy, are the major ways of attacking a problem of exposition or persuasion. In World War II, for example, one of the Allies' strategic ideas was to bomb all the German ball-bearing factories. This ideas was based on the notion that without ball-bearings, no airplanes, tanks, submarines, and heavy guns could be made. This strategic idea was carried out by a whole series of supports, or tactics. The tactics, as opposed to the strategy, involved selecting certain kinds of bombs and ways and times to fly to each factory with the greatest safety and bomb with accuracy. *Strategy, then, is the overall approach to a problem. Tactics are the specific procedures for carrying out and supporting the strategy.* Thus, in a political campaign a speaker may decide to use the strategy of "It's time for a change," and the tactics may involve evidence that the incumbent has not approached the problems of the day with sufficient energy or skill or has been guilty of corruption or is working on the wrong kinds of problems. *The strategy of the speech consists of the main ideas, the large blocks of subject matter, and the general statements of the speech. The tactics, on the other hand, are the specific materials, the evidence, the examples, the "proof."* (*Proof* appears in quotation marks because, strictly speaking, one cannot "prove" anything, even that you or I exist. To prove something requires us to use as proof materials that cannot, themselves, be proved. For example, Euclid's *Geometry* "proves" all manner of theorems. The theorems, however, are "proved" from axioms, postulates and definitions, such as "A straight line is the shortest distance between two points," that cannot themselves be proved. How could you prove that a straight line *is* the shortest distance between two points? If you try to do it by putting two points on a sheet of paper and then challenging someone to draw a shorter line between the points than the one that directly connects them, does the fact that no one can create a shorter line prove the idea? No, because you cannot show that there are not two points, somewhere in the universe, between which a straight line is not the shortest distance. In fact, in space over great distances, because space is "warped," sometimes a straight line is *not* the shortest distance between two points. Although we need to be skeptical about the use of the word proof, we can be sure that proof is supporting material—that is, material supporting general statements.)

It is well to understand the difference between general statements and support because their properties are different: First of all, general statements, or ideas by themselves, are often dull. The firm support of tactics is necessary to make ideas effective and interesting. The strategy, or idea, is an assertion, a point, a general statement, a conclusion that the speaker wants the audience to believe. Strategy is, of course, of obvious importance. The main points of a speech determine where the energy of the speech will be directed. Yet strategy itself has certain properties that make it ineffective, except in the hands of a master. *Points or generalities are not interesting of themselves.* "We need a better Pure Food and Drug Act" is probably not interesting to you unless you know some of the specific problems and dangers that lead to the idea. General statements, ideas, assertions, points (which are all synonyms for what we have called *strategy*) are often dull. These are, curiously, the important parts of the speech, but they are, at first, often the least interesting. Suppose one avoids the general statement about a Pure Food and Drug Act and, instead of stating the general idea, begins a speech as follows:

> Before our present Pure Food and Drug Act, a popular toothpaste in the United States contained a deadly poison! Yet this toothpaste was used by millions who kept it in their medicine cabinets, brushed their teeth with it, and left it within the reach of children. The "regular" tube contained twelve grams of potassium chlorate; eight grams is enough to kill a man. In World War I, a German army officer committed suicide by eating the contents of a tube, and in doing so unwittingly ate one third more than his system required. Children need even less. Today there is no such toothpaste on the market. It was driven off the market by the Pure Food and Drug Act.
>
> We used to see advertisements about gargles that "have the power to kill germs," or that "can prevent flu." No known gargle can perform such feats, although it is probably true that if you suspend a cold virus or an influenza virus in one of those gargles, the poor viruses will probably starve to death. However, gargles can neither reach nor control all the viruses responsible for

influenza. After a long battle with the producers of these gargles, the Food and Drug Administration was able to prevent such advertisements. Today people no longer are urged by advertising to spend money for such purposes and to depend on gargles when they should depend on medical care. Without a Pure Food and Drug Act, companies would still be making money selling mouthwashes by fraudlant advertising.

But all is not yet well, because we still find corrupt practices involving food and drugs. We find pills that are advertised "for morning backache," toothpastes that are said "to whiten your teeth," and ointments that are said to stop "burning and itching." Well, they generally don't work, and we need a better Pure Food and Drug Act to stop unethical companies from robbing the buyer.

Note that the tactics made the idea that we need a better Pure Food and Drug Act more interesting. *The support, not the idea, created interest and got attention.* We might create still more interest in the idea if we gave more examples of dangerous products or of advertising that makes false claims. The point is, our audience's attention and interest are captured by our examples, not by our basic idea.

Why is the concrete clear and interesting and the general dull? It is difficult to know why. Indeed, among informed people, general ideas are often quite interesting, but unless you are certain that your audience is informed about your subject and already interested in it, you must rely on tactics to develop their interest. Perhaps general ideas are dull for the reason that the noted physicist, the late James Jeans gave in *Physics and Philosophy*. He believed that because our nervous systems evolved from a long line of fish and quadrupeds, it is more suited to perceiving the concrete items of the world than to mulling over abstractions. To survive, all our forerunners had to *sense* the animal crouching to spring or *see* and *hear* the smaller animal that would be the source of the next meal. Those who could perceive these concrete data easily and quickly survived, and those who could not perished. The survivors passed on to their descendents, to us, the secret of their survival: a nervous system that makes it easy to perceive and be interested in concrete things. Only recently in our existence has the perception of ideas, of high-order abstractions, or of abstract truths been important; hence, our nervous system is still better suited to perceiving the concrete rather than the abstract. Because our survival now depends more on sensing the importance of ideas than it used to, perhaps we will develop the same sensitivity to ideas that we have to concrete things. However, such development may take millions of years and, perhaps, may never take place. At any rate, people find the concrete, the specific, more interesting than the abstract, and we do not know, for sure, why.

Whatever the reason, audiences will nearly always listen more attentively to vivid examples and concrete instances than to general statements. Speakers who recognize this truth will set about preparing for a speech differently from those who do not. They will struggle with the subject to reduce it to the fewest possible general statements, each of which will be indispensable; they will, especially, search diligently to find a barrage of specific supporting material: illustrations, instances, statistics, narratives, and analogies. This specific supporting material will nearly always be more clear and much more vivid than general statements. Whether or not the audience will be interested in what the speaker says depends on his or her supporting material.

Because general material is dull and supporting material is (if well used) interesting, we must keep aware of the differences between the two kinds of material. Moreover, we should learn to distinguish between the two because general material, although dull, is basic to what we want the audience to remember and therefore is more important than supporting material. In the distinction between general and supporting material lies the indispensable tools for successful speaking and successful writing. This difference in the interest values and the importance of these two parts of the basic unit of discourse suggests some important procedures in speech making:

1. *Strive to prepare speeches that consist largely of supporting material:* statistics, examples, analogies, testimony, summaries, and visual aids. These materials are the most interesting to audiences.

2. *Strive to prepare speeches that have only a few carefully selected general statements.* Because the statements must be kept at a minimum, each one must be indispensable to the subject chosen.

Good speaking, then consists of finding the right ideas for strategy and the maximum amount of good supporting tactics to give those ideas interest and clarity. Let us see how the informative speaker—and later the persuasive speaker—can use tactics and strategy.

Exercises

1. The ideal of the Renaissance was that one should know everything that was important and be able to perform every worthwhile skill well. If you were to try to be a Renaissance person today, name five magazines that it would be worthwhile to read. Explain your choices.

2. Is there any way you might select books to buy so that you might come as close as possible to being a Renaissance person? Explain. What kinds of books would you omit? Explain.

3. Find some anthologies of essays in the library. Read four or five of the essays. Write a composition on "Why the contemporary essay (magazine article) is (is not) our century's most important art form."

4. Read all the editorials in today's newspaper. Describe the use of the basic unit of discourse in one of them. Which kind of material predominates? Is the editorial interesting or dull? Explain why by referring to the parts of the basic unit of discourse.

5. Describe the best college lecture you have heard. Why was it the best?

6. Think of the worst lecturer you have heard. What made the person the worst? Explain.

7. Find ten magazine articles that draw a conclusion, such as "Such and such a product will . . . ." What supporting material is used? Is the material interesting? Is it valid support of the conclusion?

8. Examine a candidate's campaign speech. What are the conclusions the candidate draws? What is the support used for the conclusion? Evaluate the support.

3

Support:
The Tactics
of Exposition

NAPOLEON AVOWED THAT poor strategy followed by sound tactics is stronger than the best strategy supported by poor tactics. Something of the same is true in expository speaking. We have already seen that tactics—supporting material—can make ideas clear and interesting. We must spend much time discovering support for ideas. Sometimes we may be forgiven for selecting a less-than-crucial main point; if it is supported brilliantly, the audience may respond with interest. To locate the best supporting material, we must be thoroughly familiar with the kinds of support available for exposition. Five kinds that are most frequently used in exposition will be emphasized: statistics, examples, analogies, summaries, and visual aids. (Testimony will be omitted until Chapter 6.)

Statistics

Statistics can inject a powerful element of interest into a speech, but a speaker must often work with statistics to make them as interesting as possible. The mere recitation of statistics is apt to bore an audience. There are, however, some ways of making statistics clear and meaningful so that they add both interest and vividness to a speech. We will discuss some ways to make statistics interesting and effective.

Breaking Statistics into Comprehensible Units

One billion dollars is more money than a human being can comprehend. If we want to impress an audience with the size of such a sum, we can do so by breaking the sum into smaller units that can be comprehended, as in the following:

> How much is a billion dollars? If you started in business in the year A.D. 1 with a billion dollars in capital and managed that business so poorly that it lost $1,000 a day, how long could you stay in business? $1,000 a day is much more than most of us will ever make—or, I hope, lose. But if you had started two thousand years ago, would you still have been in business when the Roman Empire ended four hundred years later? Yes. Would you have been in business by the time of the first crusade, over a thousand years after you started losing money? Yes. You would still have been in business on the day the Civil War ended, and you would be in business right now. And you could stay in business without making a single dime, losing $1,000 a day for another seven hundred years. That's how much a billion dollars is.

Thus, we can help others understand an apparently incomprehensibly large figure by imaginatively breaking it into smaller, more comprehensible units. The best way to master the technique of dramatizing statistics that are too large to comprehend is to practice techniques of breaking them into meaningful units in interesting ways. Suppose, for example, that you want to dramatize the number of miles between the earth and the sun—93,000,000 miles. You might use any number of methods: You might calculate how long it would take the fastest plane to fly the distance, or how long it would take to drive the distance in a car. But these ways, although they would make the statistic meaningful, are too obvious to be as intrinsically interesting as some more original techniques might be. Some less obvious methods of dramatizing the distance from here to the sun follow:

1. Calculate the number of gallons of gasoline a car would need to make the trip, and tell how many railroad tank cars (which hold 50,000 gallons each) you would have to take with you to make the trip.

2. If you were to attempt to walk the distance, how many generations would it take?

3. If the average pair of shoes lasts for 1,500 miles of walking, how many shoes would you have to take along to walk from the earth to the sun? Because dividing 1,500 into 93,000,000 will still yield a figure that is not very comprehensible, make the unit larger, perhaps as follows: A large shoe store may have about 1,000 pairs of shoes. How many of these shoe stores in your size would you have to take along to walk from the earth to the sun? (The answer: enough shoes to fill 930,000 large shoe stores—all in your size. It's a long walk!)

A speaker must try a variety of methods of dramatizing figures and then select those ways that are most effective. Never be satisfied with the first technique you hit on; it is likely to be mediocre. Find different ways of dramatizing the figure by breaking it into comprehensible units. For example, find ten ways of dramatizing a given statistic that is too large to comprehend (and this kind of statistic is the only kind for which this technique is suitable—don't try to use it on comprehensible statistics such as percentages or small numbers). Then select the three or four best ways to dramatize it. You will be selecting the best of several ways of making the figure dramatic, delivering a barrage of ways to the audience. If one way doesn't work well on some members of the audience, you still have other methods that may. But above all, when you have a statistic that is so large that it is difficult to comprehend, make the figure impressive by breaking it up into meaningful units in a variety of original ways. When you do so, the figure will not bore your audience; it will impress them.

Interspersing Statistics with Other Material

It is not uncommon for inexperienced speakers to misuse statistics by relying entirely on them. Even well-dramatized statistics can become dull if they are over used. Guard against making speeches that are overly statistical, not only because they lack variety and fail to be as interesting as they might, but because you should be able to grasp the *human aspects* of the matter about which you speak. A speaker who uses statistics well may become careless and neglect to reflect the more human aspects of the situation. As speakers, and as human beings, we have the responsibility of grasping more than the statistical elements of the subject. We do not really understand starvation in India, for example, if all we know is the figures for agricultural production, the figures for exports and imports, the number of calories the average person receives, and the like. We have failed to grasp the situation *from the standpoint of someone in that situation.* Thus, in using statistics, be careful to interject other forms of support to sustain interest by adding variety. It is especially important for us intelligent speakers to catch and reflect an understanding of the human aspects of the situations we are discussing. To reflect the human aspects of a situation, use another form of support: the example.

Hypothetical Examples

The hypothetical example is one that is supposed or imagined but that did not actually happen. Good hypothetical examples may often achieve an effect that cannot be achieved otherwise. For example, the following is part of a hypothetical example:

> Imagine that through some act—a mistake, an act that starts as a bluff, or an act of insanity—some nation decides to drop its largest nuclear bombs on our cities and our defense installations. What will happen to you on that day? What will happen to your friends and your family? What will happen to the country?

An opening has been made for a good hypothetical example that will enable the audience to visualize a situation that has not yet happened, and we hope never will. But to help the audience experience something that has not happened is not easy. To work out the rest of this hypothetical illustration (I suggest you try to complete it before going on) requires ability that most college students have; it requires however, in addition, artistry, imagination, and plain hard work. For example, if you were to complete the illustration begun above, you might want to ask yourself some of the following questions; keep in mind that some of these may lead to helpful materials:

1. If the bomb were dropped today at noon, where would most of the members of the class be?
2. If the bomb were dropped on your city, what might be the landmark that would be the focus of the explosion?
3. How large an area around you would be destroyed from that focus with bombs of various sizes—from one megaton to twenty megatons? (You'll need to visit the library to look up the answer to this question.)
4. Although they would eventually die of radiation poisioning how far from the focus would people have to be to avoid instant death?
5. What would be the influence on the survivors' habits of eating, working, recreation, medical care, and the like?
6. Read some works about the atom bombing of Japan, such as John Hersey's *Hiroshima*, for some eye-witness accounts of the effects of the bomb; incorporate similar items in your hypothetical account.
7. Plan, during your speech to ask the audience questions such as some of the above about the bombing and their family.
8. Daydream about what might happen in a nuclear attack; such day-dreaming can be productive, and is often used by good speakers to help them get ideas.
9. Read about the effects of bombing; compare the characteristics of the atomic fission bomb, atomic fusion bomb, cobalt bomb, neutron bomb, and the like. Each has terrifyingly different effects that will make your example more powerful.
10. Develop more material than you can use, and then select the best of what you've collected for the hypothetical illustration.

If you work enough on the example, you should be able to describe vividly the devastation of familiar buildings, districts, parks, and other public areas, you will be able to describe the devastation for members of your audience, perhaps even making a good guess as to where the audience might be when the bomb went off. You might paint a picture of the slow death that would come to those who escaped instant vaporization by the bomb—how the feeling of weakness, the loss of hair and teeth, and the onslaught of nausea, wretching, and vomiting preceed death, and how the final hours of death would come. You can see that to compose such an example and make it good will take time. Some speakers enjoy spending the time, some are willing to spend the time whether they enjoy it or not, and others are unwilling to do the work. To those who are unwilling, I strongly recommend finding good real examples and not hypothetical ones. A dull hypothetical example puts an audience to sleep, and it's difficult to awaken them. A good, well worked out hypothetical example can help an audience to visualize events that may not yet have occurred, to sense the horror—or delight—in what you are recommending, and to enliven your ideas.

In using hypothetical examples, do not, of course, "invent" an example and pass it off as real. Hypothetical examples are effective even when they describe an impossible situation, but always be sure to include the signposts of a hypothetical example: "Imagine that . . ." or "Let's suppose . . . ."

Writing Vivid Examples

The difference between a dull and a vivid example is that the vivid example, whether it is real or hypothetical, often incorporates one or more of the following devices: (1) vivid description, (2) characterization, and (3) narration. Let us see what these devices are and how they can be used to increase the vividness of real and hypothetical examples.

VIVID DESCRIPTION. Vivid description uses imagery. An image is a representation by symbols of something the senses can perceive directly. A vivid example of a slum area would use words that represent the sounds, sights, and feelings of one perceiving a slum. If one picture is worth a thousand words, the strongest words are images—for images are words (symbols) that stand for pictures and arouse pictures in the minds of the audience. Thus, if you are concerned about poverty, you must describe what poverty presents to the senses; if you want your audience to drive safely, describe an accident with all its vivid imagery; if you want your audience to help stop air pollution, describe how air pollution looks and smells, and, perhaps, contrast the scene with a description of life before polluted air became a problem; if you want to encourage slum clearance, describe with vivid imagery what slums look like, sound like, smell like, and feel like. Let us take a specific example here: Suppose you are giving a speech on the theme "Religious beliefs can be dangerous." To the novice speaker, this subject may not appear to lend itself to imagery. Yet, the discerning student will see that it does. You might decide to select the following idea as one of the main points: "Self-righteously religious people often persecute those who differ with them." With this as the main point, you must now look for supporting material. The best bet will be to look for historical examples. Have there ever been times when self-righteousness has led to the persecutions of others? Persecutions sponsored by Catholics, Protestants, Jews, Buddhists, and Moslems, can be immediately recalled; indeed, it is a rare religion that has not both practiced and experienced persecution. One of the more senseless persecutions might furnish you with an example to open your speech. If you were to choose the persecution of the Huguenots, you might decide to describe an episode in their persecution using images of sight, sound, and pain. The result might provide a vivid introduction to your ideas:

> Religious bigotry leads to the opposite of what all great religions stand for: It leads to oppression instead of charity, distrust instead of understanding, hate instead of love, taking life instead of saving it. One of the bloodiest examples of bigotry was the attempt to destroy the Huguenots in the sixteenth and seventeenth centuries. Over 30,000 of them were killed, many by

crucifixion. You have never seen a man crucified, and probably never will. But if you had watched one of them being crucified, it might have been like this:

If you stood at the foot of the cross as it lay on the ground, you would have seen five soldiers do their work in fewer than five minutes. First the soldiers held the victim—a Huguenot—on the cross. Then one soldier drove a wooden peg through the victim's right wrist; then one through his left; then one through both feet. Each peg had to be hammered hard until it sank deep into the wood beneath. The cross was then erected, and as the sun sank beneath the earth, this cross, silhouetted in black against a crimson sky, stood with thousands of others as testimony to the devoutness of France; for all this was done in the name of righteousness and Christ.

There is almost no subject for which imagery cannot be used to advantage. A speech favoring tariff reduction can describe the way such reduction stimulates trade and business; it lends itself to the imagery of busy machines and factories. A speech advocating better study methods can describe the feelings of frustration, disappointment, and even terror in the student who fails because he or she uses ineffective skills. Some subjects, of course, lend themselves to the use of imagery more than others, but *wherever a speaker uses examples, the possibility arises of using images to increase the vividness of the example.* Let us consider some suggestions for using good imagery in writing:

1. Use the varieties of imagery best suited to the subject. Imagery is more than a "picture," because the term *imagery* includes not only things that can be seen, but things that can be heard and felt. A reasonably useful and diverse classification of kinds of imagery includes the following:

Visual Imagery: Symbols standing for things that can be seen

Auditory Imagery: Symbols standing for things that can be heard

Gustatory Imagery: Symbols standing for things that can be tasted

Tactile Imagery: Symbols standing for things that can be touched, such as rough and smooth surfaces, dampness, and dryness

Olfactory Imagery: Symbols standing for things that can be smelled

Kinesthetic Imagery: Symbols standing for the sense of movement

Thermal Imagery: Symbols standing for the sensations of heat and cold

Pain Imagery: Symbols standing for physical pain

Organic Imagery: Symbols standing for internal sensations, such as depression, elation, and nausea

2. Describe only items that can be directly sensed. If you are describing a slum, you are *not* using imagery if you say, "The houses were old and tumble-down looking." Such a statement is *a conclusion drawn from what you might perceive and is not the series of sense perceptions that led to your conclusion.* The conclusion that the houses were old and tumble-down looking lacks vividness, and the able user of images reduces such conclusions to a minimum. *Much more vivid are the discrete bits of sense data that led to the conclusion:* a broken window was stuffed with newspapers to keep out the cold; a screen door, with the bottom of the screen rusted away, hung on its one remaining hinge and angrily banged in the wind.

In *The Light That Failed*, Rudyard Kipling has an artist describe painting as a process in which you see with uncommon sharpness and then return to your studio, to remember better than you ever saw. The writing of images is much the same. You must learn to *see and remember the sensory matters that led to a conclusion.* Or, to put it in another way, instead of looking at a *group* of houses, look at *just one* board, or *just one* step and describe *only* what you see, avoiding conclusions wherever possible. Thus, you should not say "The child was dirty," you should describe what about the child led to your conclusion. Rather than say, "The street was filthy," you should describe with some precision what you saw that led to your conclusion. Fresh, original, vivid imagery is in part developed by looking carefully at specific items—a single window, a door, board, a step—and describing *only* what you sense directly.

CHARACTERIZATION.   Vivid examples often can make use of characterization to enhance their effect. An example may be strengthened if it contains one or more clearly discernible characters selected to achieve some of the following effects:

1. Depict a person with whom the audience can identify. We identify with those who are like us: those who have the same basic aims, customs, status, frustrations, blunders, and foibles. Thus, a character must be represented as similar to the audience in one or more ways. Often this similarity can be simply and quickly depicted:

> Abdul is a Moslem and lives in a different culture with different customs. He wears an Arabian headdress and bows to Mecca. *But being about your age, he likes most of the things you like.* Of course, he doesn't own a car, but he has seen many of them. He doesn't go to school, as you do. He will remain illiterate and work at jobs that are given to illiterates. But like all people, he gets hungry when he hasn't eaten—just as you do. Like you, one day he will start a family; but unlike you, he won't be able to support them. And, unlike you, he will see those starve who lack a job or the skill at thievery to escape hunger.

Far less effective would be the same matter put in general terms, without the character; the audience will only mildly identify with the subject:

> Moslems in the Middle East have a different culture and different customs. Their clothes are different, their religion is different. But they like, want, and need many of the things you do. They have seen cars, and they know about schools, although they may never have been in either.

Without a character with whom the audience can identify, the passage is less apt to get a response. Often the response of readers to fiction and of audiences to plays and motion pictures is based partly on the change in attitude that occurs when the audience identifies with the leading character of the story, or disidentifies with or rejects one who represents the opposite of what the author wishes the audience to accept. Thus the character in an example with whom the audience can identify, either positively or negatively, may contribute to the vividness of the example.

2. A second effect of characterization is that of personification. One may select or create a character who illustrates a way of life, a point of view, a characteristic. Literature is full of such personifications. Thus Uriah Heep personifies the use of a false and assumed humility in order to "raise one's station." Lady Macbeth personifies grasping, reckless ambition. Othello personifies one who "loved not wisely, but too well." Personification enables the writer to show how a general principle applies in a specific case. Thus, through Uncle Tom, we see the application of slavery, just as through the characters in *Death of a Salesman*, and especially the character of Willie Loman, we see the way a salesman may live and die. We may not *identify* with a person who *personifies* a point of view, but we can get a concrete picture of that point of view as it impinges on human life.

Good characterization in a speech, therefore, requires one to find or create characters with which the audience can *identify* or who *personify* concretely an attitude, force, or way of life.

NARRATIVE. Stories have held the interest of people for thousands of years. Everyone likes a good story, and when a good narrative can be used in a speech, it will help to hold attention. But what is a story? The broadest meaning of *narrative* is the depiction of changes. In this sense, one might write a narrative of a city and depict its founding, growth, decay, and renewal. More strictly, narrative goes beyond mere change, becoming *change as a result of the conflict of forces*. The typical story is a study of the conflict of persons—the hero and the villain—or a study of the conflict of a person against an impersonal force—such as a person against fate or destiny. Such narratives increase the possibilities for capturing the audience's attention, for they permit the use of identification, of personification, of suspense, of concrete interpretation of a theme, and of intrinsically interesting action. The novels of Charles Dickens were persuasive: they were a powerful force that resulted in better legislation to protect the rights of children. Quite probably, *Uncle Tom's Cabin* was not great literature, but it was effective in showing people the evil of slavery and in keeping England from supporting the Confederacy; quite possibly, the story was more effective than statistical demonstrations, the use of informed testimony, or other more "logical" means. Just so, brief stories or vignettes included in a speech can make a point with compelling vividness. Therefore, try to discover or create narrative examples that will make your points both clear and vivid to an audience.

Instances

An instance is a form of real example, but it is a very short form. Sometimes it involves only the name of an example. Yet, such instances, when they are well chosen, can be compelling. Consider the following:

> People say that Socialism leads to Communism. Why is it, then, that the socialist countries are the *least* in danger of becoming communistic? Among the more stable countries in the world are Norway, Austria, Sweden, Denmark, England, New Zealand, and Australia, all of which are socialistic, but none of which is in danger of becoming communistic.

The idea that socialism—of a particular form—does not lead to Communism is here supported with the mere names of examples. As such, instances are effective because they can supply an enormous amount of information in a short time. But the instance is not by itself very interesting. There is nothing in the preceding series of instances that is interest catching. The instance will be vivid *only* when it is (1) used to attack a commonly held belief or (2) used to support an idea that has already captured the interest of the audience. Unless you are certain the audience will be deeply interested in the idea you intend to support by instances, you had better stimulate their interest first by using vivid examples. Then the use of instances may be valuable in clinching your point.

Analogies

The analogy is a special form of the example that attempts to show that something that is true in one circumstance may be true under similar circumstances. For example, why the sky is blue can be explained by the use of an analogy with waves of the ocean:

> You have stood at the shore of a lake or ocean and watched the waves come in. You have noticed that tiny waves, when they hit an obstacle, such as an old post in the water, are bounced—reflected back—but the large waves roll over the obstacle and continue their course. Light, too, can be thought of as the motion of waves. The long waves—those at the red end of the spectrum—"roll" over the obstacles they encounter. But the shorter waves—those at the blue end of the spectrum—are reflected by the tiny dust particles that fill our atmosphere. From these dust particles, the blue light is reflected so that it enters our eyes from every angle of the sky and makes the sky look blue.

The analogy can often make ideas both clear and striking. Analogies can also make an idea more believable. After Galileo discovered moons circulating around Jupiter, many people, on the analogy of bodies rotating about a planet, were willing to consider the idea that the earth revolved about the sun. Many an election campaign has been won—and lost—on the old analogy "Don't change horses in the middle of a stream." Although some analogies are not logically strong, as we will see in the section on rhetorical logic, even these kinds can help make an idea clear and striking.

Analogical thinking is much more pervasive than one might think. We often conceive of complicated things by using an analogy that we call a model. Thus, the early behaviorists conceived of the brain as containing a telephone switchboard that connected the parts of the brain: the part on which optical phenomena were interpreted could be connected with the part that "remembered", so that what we saw would be retained by the brain. But more modern thinking conceives of the brain as a kind of "transformer" that changes the raw data of our experience into symbols; such symbols occur in our dreams and in our use of language. To understand the brain by making it analogous to a telephone switchboard gives one kind of understanding of the brain; to see it as a transformer will lead us to different conclusions. For a while, it seemed that the brain was like a computer, but even this way of conceiving it was far too limited; we lack a good model for the brain, and partly because of this fact, the brain still baffles us and frustrates our attempts to understand it.

Thus, the analogy by which we learn about things influences the way we think about them. There is an enormous difference in the kinds of research done by those who conceive of the human being on the analogy of a machine and those who do not. An-alogical thought enters into many forms of understanding. In physics, light has been conceived of on the analogy of both waves and particles—both seem useful, but each is only partly correct. In economics, some have conceived of wealth as a kind of apple that can only be divided in certain ways; other, more modern, economists insist that wealth is a kind of balloon that can be inflated or deflated to increase or decrease wealth. *The model used to conceive of an idea is so important that it often conditions and changes the things we can know and do with the idea. We must, therefore, become aware of the implied analogy behind our conceptions, for the analogy sets the conditions of thought and action.*

Summaries

A summary does not, of course, add any logical strength to a speech, but it is surprising how a careful and intelligent summary—especially when it is well developed—can roll a major unit or an entire speech into a small, superpotent pellet and clinch what might otherwise be ineffective. Summaries are used too infrequently, especially by beginning speakers. It is possible to overuse summaries, but this writer, who has heard thousands of speeches, does not recall a single instance of such overuse. Plan to summarize carefully and frequently.

There are a number of ways to summarize. Plan to use one or more of the following ways, which in general are arranged in order from the least to the most effective.

Initial Summary or Forecast

Tell the audience what the major points of the speech will be at the outset of the speech. Then the audience can follow the speech more easily.

Final Summary

Review the major points at the end of the speech. If the audience has forgotten them, the review will help them remember.

Repetition

Mark Antony, in Shakespeares *Julius Caesar*, repeats "Brutus is an honourable man" several times in his speech for Caesar's burial. His use of the same words changes meaning as he goes on. Whenever meanings change or intensify, you can summarize using repetition of the same words. But if such a summary would become unnecessarily repetitious, you might want to use *different* words for the same idea. In either event, you can hardly use too many summaries. Repeat your ideas often, and such repetition will contribute to clarity.

Evidential Summary

Summarize the conclusions you have drawn, but include in the summary some of the most significant evidence for the conclusion. For example: "Studies of identical twins who were raised in not only separate but also very different environments show that these twins had corresponding differences in IQ; we can, therefore, conclude that environment influences intelligence." Such a summary is far more effective than merely reiterating the conclusion.

Cumulative Summary

The cumulative summary is particularly strong when you want the audience to *remember* your major points. After making each point, carefully summarize each preceding point, so that, at the end of point two, you are summarizing both points one and two, and at the end of point three, you are summarizing points one, two and three, and so on.

A caution about the use of summaries is required, however: the summary must not be haphazard, ineptly done, or poorly delivered. The summary, if it is to be effective, must be phrased with great care so that it is both efficient and strong; it must be delivered in such a way that the audience catches the spirit and significance entailed in the summary. A muddled summary delivered in a let-down spirit that trails off into a mumble will only subtract effectiveness from the speech.

Visual Aids

Visual aids can often ensure the vividness as well as the clarity of a speech. Objects, charts, diagrams, graphs, pictures, drawings, photographs, models, and implements can add to the attention values of the speech. A simple and well-prepared graph clarifies relationships and demonstrates trends more quickly than spoken words. But visual aids can contribute more than clarity; because they can be chosen for their novelty and vividness, and because they can be used skillfully to create suspense, they are intrinsically interesting and markedly increase the attention values of the speech.

Certain commonsense rules should be observed in connection with visual aids:

1. Make the visual aid an integral part of the speech; Do not include it merely to hold attention. If you begin an exposition of one of the causes of crime by pulling out a gun, it will hold attention; but the gun obviously is not required and is being used *merely* to hold attention. You then would be guilty both of using a trick to hold attention and of introducing the speech in a childish way that suggests that you have the kind of mind that fits the childish technique. The object should add something more to the speech than its attention value and must not be so sensational that it distracts from the speech itself.

2. Conceal the visual aid before it is needed and remove it after you use it so that it will not distract the audience from the message.
3. Practice the speech using the visual aid, until you can simultaneously speak and use it. There are at least two dangers you will face: The first is that while you write figures on the board or otherwise manipulate the visual aid chosen, there will be "dead spots" in the speech: places where it will be difficult to use the visual aids and talk at the same time. If you have not practiced, you will be unable to do both at once; the audiences attention is apt to be lost if you have not developed the facility for filling in dead spots. You may find, in addition, that unless you have practiced the speech carefully, you will mishandle the visual aid. In explaining, for example, how a booby trap works, it would be upsetting to announce: "There are three main parts to the typical booby trap" and, as you twist part of the trap, have a few bolts drop to the floor and a spring shoot out into the audience, dismantling the implement.
4. The visual aid must be large enough to be seen easily by all the members of the audience. To select an object that cannot be seen beyond the first row is amateurish.
5. Arrange the visual aid on a stand, pin it to a board, or hold it up so that the audience can see it without effort.

Exercises

1. Explain, using techniques not found in the text, how to make clear the size of the solar system by "reducing" its size: Imagine the sun to be the size of a beach ball. How far from it would the earth be? How large would Jupiter be? How far from the sun would Pluto, the farthest planet, be?

2. Explain, using techniques not found in the text, how to make clear the size of a mollecule by "expanding" its size. If a carbon atom were the size of a marble, how large would a molecule of petroleum be?

3. Take the current amount annually spent on armaments, or the current total national and state debt, and find ten ways to break the figure into comprehensible units. What three ways are best? Why?

4. Because breaking something into comprehensible units increases the apparent size of a statistic, try some devices to make the size of the statistics in Exercise 3 here appear to be smaller.

5. What single idea do you consider most important? Write a hypothetical illustration to support that idea. Use imagery, characterization—both for identification and personification—and narration to make the idea clear, interesting, and reasonable. Why does a hypothetical example work—or not work?

6. Which of the following do you consider the more accurate conception: Is wealth like a pie—there is only so much to go around—or like a balloon that can be expanded? Is the eye like a camera, or is the camera like an eye? Is the human mind like a computer? If so, in what ways? What can the mind do that the computer can't? What can the computer do that the mind can't?

7. Find four newspaper editorials. Write a clear, accurate final summary for each. Now write a cumulative summary of all that could be given after the last subpoint is made. Could an evidential summary be written for each? Why?

8. Write a summary for each of four college lectures you have heard. The summaries should make it possible for you to pass an examination on the lectures. What kinds of summaries did you use?

4

Main Ideas: The Strategy of Exposition

The Uses of Strategy

No general can devise strategy without knowledge of the terrain, the nature and number of the forces on both sides, the location of those forces, the kinds of equipment both sides have, and the strengths and weaknesses of both sides. Neither can you discover the best strategy for a speech without a thorough knowledge of the subject. You must know the subject well enough so that you can be authoritative; you must know the significance of various ideas and their probable effects on the audience; you must know the audience's state of mind, its knowledge of the subject, and its awareness of opposing ideas. Only if you have a broad and deep understanding of these things can you choose the best possible strategic ideas.

Beginning students find the selection of strategy difficult, for an understandable reason: They do not, at this point in their education, command a broad and deep view of the subjects on which they speak. So serious is the student's lack of knowledge sometimes that, at worst, the beginning speaker may not have *any* choice in strategy because he or she knows barely enough about the subject to fill the allotted time. But the facilities for gathering information today are so vast that if you make use of libraries efficiently, you can easily find good sources of information. These sources, together with the possibility of consulting experts on campus and in the community, offer you the possibility of developing breadth and depth. *But the clearest prerequisite to developing good strategy is that you must have the most thorough knowledge possible of the subject in order to be able to have a variety of choices available.*

USE FEW MAIN POINTS.   Assuming that you prepare well enough so that you have an array of large blocks of subject matter that might be included in your speech, a few suggestions may help: First of all, *strive to keep your main points few in number.* From what has already been said we can see why you must not have too many main points: These main points are, by their nature, general statements, and general statements tend to be less interesting, less clear, and less valid than supporting material. If the audience is not to be anesthetized, you must be able to distill *only* those general statements that are *crucial* to the subject. Such an act of distillation is a feat of genuine intellectual skill. It not only is an achievement of which you may be proud, but it also performs at least two functions that make the speech more successful: First, such distillation reduces general statements to an absolute essential minimum and helps an audience to comprehend the speech in the most efficient manner. If you have incorporated six major general ideas into a six-minute speech, you are naïvely expecting that the audience will understand, perhaps remember, and be influenced by ideas that you are taking only one minute to present. To stamp in an idea so that it will *influence* generally takes more than one minute. Therefore, the more ideas you decide to use in a speech, the less effective each of them will be. The best speakers generally limit severely the number of ideas that require support and will support those selected fully and powerfully, until the audience understands, believes, remembers, and is influenced by the carefully selected ideas. Second, such distillation often subtly suggests to an audience that you are a sharp-minded person who truly understands your subject. One reason student speakers are often only listened to politely is that their choice of strategy is so inept that they not only bore their audience, but advertise their ignorance. Distilling a subject down to the fewest possible directly supportable general statements not only opens the possibility for incorporating a maximum amount of dramatic, compelling supporting material, but also suggests, rightly, something about the intellectual competence of the speaker.

STATE POINTS VIVIDLY.   In addition to being few in number, *main points should be stated as vividly as possible.* The inexperienced speaker usually cannot write vivid main points without effort. You must check over your speech to be sure that your main points are as strongly stated as they deserve to be. Write and rewrite them, constantly removing unnecessary words and substituting more precise and more vigorous language, until at last you have them phrased in a way that will make it easy for the audience to grasp immediately and to remember.

Using vivid language in phrasing your general statements is a skill that, although important, seems to develop late in most speakers. Usually the beginning speaker soon develops the ability to use supporting material well but not the ability to write general statements that are clear and vivid by themselves. Yet, this skill is important to the speaker because a vividly written general statement is easily perceived by the audience and may influence them without the need of long additions of examples. Some speakers and writers habitually state their points vividly and can be understood *without* the addition of frequent illustrations.

In the *Philosophy of Style*, Herbert Spencer, the nineteenth century philosopher, illustrates some interesting techniques for writing generalizations. Consider the following illustration of a general statement that is difficult to understand the first time it is read: "In proportion as the customs and diversions of human societies are cruel and barbarous, so will the regulations of their penal code be severe." Far better is the following statement, which is at once both clear and vivid: "As we delight in bullfights and gladiatorial combats, so will we punish by hanging, burning, and the rack." The second statement, although it uses fewer words than the first, is a far better statement than the first.

What difference accounts for the merit of the second statement? The difference is that the second statement uses a specific instance of the general principle, instead of stating the principle itself. In the second statement, instead of saying "customs and diversions of human societies," the writer substitutes instances of those customs and diversions: "bullfights and gladiatorial combats." Instead oof using general language for "so will the regulations of their penal code be severe," the second statement again substitutes specific instances of severe regulations: "so will we punish by hanging, burning, and the rack." Thus, *one way of writing vivid general principles is to cast them in language that substitutes specific instances for the general ideas.*

The classic example of a speaker who wrote general statements so brilliantly that many of his statements became slogans is Ralph Waldo Emerson. (Most of his published essays, by the way, were first delivered as lectures.) The following general statements are inept paraphrases of some ideas he presented in "The American Scholar." Try to rephrase the following paragraph so that it is at once vivid and clear:

> Information accumulated by others involves the abeyant periods of one's own productivity. This accumulation serves to increase the possibilities for creative motivation. Books, which should be means to greater ends, often become merely ends in themselves. The result is the pretentious collaborator who accumulates and publishes indexes of other people's contributions. Our institutions of higher learning can best meet the needs of society if they can accumulate the various contributions to human thought of creative minorities with the end in view that these works can be used to further implement additional discoveries and insights.

Before reading the following "Emersonian" expression of these ideas, try yourself to substitute specific and vivid words for the general principles expressed. After trying for ten or fifteen minutes, you will most likely give up, for few men had Emerson's ability to epitomize a general idea by substituting for it a specific and vivid word:

> Books are for the scholar's idle times. They serve for nothing but to inspire. But the worship of the hero corrupts into the worship of the statue, and so we have the bibliomaniac, the bookworm. Our colleges can serve us best when they gather within their hospitable walls all the concentrated fires of genius and set the hearts of youth aflame.

Both compositions are on the idea that learning must inspire. Yet, one is clear and vivid, and achieves this vividness with few words; the other is prolix, dull, and reflects a mind that is not on fire, but only full of smoke.

SELECT POINTS FOR THE AUDIENCE. *Choose points with the audience in mind.* In speaking to an audience untutored in biology on the subject "You should study biology," you would not choose to introduce your subject with the point "Ontogeny recapitulates phylogeny." The idea would be incomprehensible to those who knew nothing of either the evolution of species or of embryology. Instead, start a speech with material that fits the level of knowledge of the audience. Furthermore, suit the choice of points to the interests of the audience and build from the interests already present in the audience toward those in which you wish to create interest. Therefore, *constantly check your main points to be sure that you have selected them so that they are within, or based on, both the level of knowledge of the audience and its interests.*

RELATE STRATEGIC POINTS TO EACH OTHER. *Select strategic ideas that, in some way, are related.* Audiences may become confused and give up their attempt to follow a speech when the units of a speech fail to bear simple and obvious relations to each other. You can. however, relate these ideas, to each other and to the central theme in a number of ways.

Select points so that they follow each other in a time or space sequence. Thus, if you are discussing the development of the central nervous system in animals, relate your ideas to a developmental sequence so that each point represents a further

development of an aspect of the nervous system; your points
might be made as follows:

1. The development of an axial nervous system into a
   spinal cord
2. The development of ganglionization or large bunches
   of nerves along the spinal cord
3. The development of encephalization or the location of
   the largest ganglion near the head of the spinal cord
4. The development of the cerebral cortex

You may, if discussing "We should abolish poverty in Appalachia," choose main points related to this theme as follows:
(1) the extent of poverty in Appalachia, (2) the causes of poverty
in Appalachia, (3) the solution to poverty in Appalachia. Here to
the relation is that of problem, cause, and solution.[1] But if you
were discussing the idea "Poverty in the world must be
reduced," you might choose, instead of a problem-solving
sequence, a *time* sequence: (1) the effects of poverty on ancient
civilizations, (2) the effects of poverty today, (3) the probable
future effects of poverty if it is not reduced, (4) the probable
future effects of treating poverty now.

To relate points to a central theme, first state that theme
carefully; then select points in such a way that all of them have a
describable relation to the theme.

You can relate to a central theme and to each other in many
different ways: from simple to complex, from known to unknown, from part to whole, from cause to effect, from problem
to solution, or in many complex variations of these relationships.
Try, however, to build into your sequence of main points some
discernible relationship.

Coordinate points should be parallel wherever possible. Parallelism often gives points of sufficient relationship to each

---

[1] For a more thorough introduction to problem solving order as well as to
problem solving itself, see Otis M. Walter, *Speaking Intelligently: Communication
for Problem Solving*, New York: Macmillan Publishing Co., 1976. See especially
the chapters "Problems," "Presenting Problems," "Causes," and "Solutions."

other to make your choice of ideas clear. Points that are parallel are usually of about equal importance and use the same grammatical pattern. The following points lack parallelism:

1. The cost of crime represents both direct and indirect expense to the taxpayer.
2. If we could rehabilitate those disposed to criminal action, we could turn many into more productive assets.

The following restatements of these ideas are parallel. (Note that these parallel restatements are much easier for the audience to grasp and remember. Note also that they will be far easier for you, the speaker, to remember.)

1. Crime wastes money.
2. Crime wastes human resources.

Parallel points are necessarily related to each other; therefore, one way to be certain the main points of a unit are related is to state them in parallel form. After you have stated your points so that they are parallel, you may want to check them again to see whether they can also be related to each other in one of the ways suggested here: simple to complex, known to unknown, and so forth. In any event, the more you can relate the ideas to each other, the more unified your speech will be. Providing unity is one way of increasing the impact of the speech. Therefore, the relating of points to each other in a speech is a powerful psychological device that increases the possibility that the speech can be remembered and will influence an audience.

In summary, take extreme care to choose your ideas for strategy carefully. Always ask yourself whether you know enough about the subject to be able to choose the best possible points; and if you do not, spend the time and effort to gather the necessary knowledge of the subject. But throughout the process of building the speech, also ask yourself the following questions about your choice of main points:

1. Are these main points so well chosen that they are few in number and indispensable to the subject?
2. Are these points stated with maximum clarity and vividness?
3. Are these points stated to reflect the knowledge and interests of the audience?
4. Are these main points related to each other in a clear and precise way?

Introductions

The minimum requirement for an introduction in an expository speech is that it capture the attention of the audience. From what has already been said, this capturing of attention often can best be done by using vivid supporting material. As a novice, especially, avoid opening with general statements, irrelevant remarks, or apologies. Because a novice is insecure, he or she often apologizes. Such apologies are unnecessary, and probably, rather than expressing regret, are a masked excuse for some failure on the part of the speaker.

The Use of Supporting Material
in the Introduction

Perhaps the best advice is to open directly with some interesting supporting material. If you are explaining the causes of inflation, for example, open with a powerful description of how inflation ruined millions in Germany after World War I; explain how a suitcase full of money was needed to buy a loaf of bread, how the German mint found it impossible to print new money fast enough and was required to print new numerals on old money to raise bills valued at a thousand marks to as much as ten thousand or a hundred thousand. Or begin with vivid examples of those living on salaries and fixed incomes who were made penniless by an inflation that reduced their purchasing power so much that they could no longer buy food. Often the easiest way

to open an informative speech is to use the strongest supporting
material you can find.

Explaining the Significance
of the Informative Material

A second way of opening the informative speech is to demonstrate the importance of the material to the audience. This kind
of introduction is much more difficult than the first, for several
reasons. First, it involves the use of general statements, which
are difficult to make interesting. Second, the importance of
many ideas is difficult to understand, and even the best speakers
may not be aware of the consequences of certain kinds of ideas.
Newton, for example, never understood the effects his ideas of
mechanics might have on religion. Descartes, the founder of
modern philosophy, did not realize that one effect of his philosophy would be to weaken the dogmatic strength of the Catholic
church. "What are the possible effects of an idea?" is a question
that only the most adventurous dare try to answer. Yet, if as a
speaker you *can* explain vividly the reasons an audience should
understand the ideas you are about to explicate, your ideas may
top sources of interest that will greatly increase both the com-
prehension of the audience and the influence you have on their
ideas. The danger of such an approach is that the speaker will
become too general, and the introduction, instead of creating
interest, will anesthetize. The experienced expository writer or
speaker can often use this kind of introduction successfully,
because experience teaches one to support every possible general statement with vivid, specific materials; however, the novice
had best stay away from it until he or she is certain about the
effect the information may have on the listeners, until he or she
can support statements about the importance of a subject with
vivid details. The best way to capture attention, especially for the
novice, is to open without general statements and plunge immediately into a barrage of vivid supporting material, such as
examples or dramatized statistics. A more experienced speaker,
however, may wish to explain the significance of the material he

or she is about to give, and in so doing may create interest that will sustain the audience's attention throughout the speech.

Conclusions

The conclusion of a speech may either be a clear summary of the ideas presented or a development of what the ideas given may mean for the future. Here again, if you are a novice it is best to end as simply and clearly as possible. Use one or more of the kinds of summaries suggested in Chapter 3.

If you are a novice, the same advice that pertains to introductions may help you work out a conclusion. You may conclude with an example that epitomizes the idea, some compelling statistics, or a story that makes the point. Additional concrete material of high interest value may, as always, provide a strong conclusion.

If you are a more experienced speaker, you may choose to compose a conclusion that states, in the strongest language possible, your position. The conclusions from Patrick Henry's "Give me liberty or give me death" speech, from Bryan's "Cross of gold" speech, from Churchill, and others, are known the world over. Few beginners have the ability to write such prose, and directions for achieving, even partially, some of the skills involved in such writing are beyond the scope of this book. If you intuitively know how to compose a powerfully climactic passage, do so. But a satisfactory conclusion can be made from either a clear summary of the major ideas of the speech or from a final but interesting item of supporting material, especially a good example or compelling story.

Exercises

1. Listen to three expository lectures; at least one of them should be a television program such as "Nova," or "National Geographic." Answer the following questions:

    a. Were summaries used? Were the summaries well used? Explain.

    b. Can you easily recall the main points of the presentations? Why?

    c. Were the main points few in number, stated with maximum clarity and vividness, stated to reflect the knowledge and interests of the audience, and related to each other in a clear and precise way?

    d. Which of the three was the best expository lecture? Why?

5
Persuasion: An Overview

The Need for Persuasion

The study of persuasion is among the oldest of all studies. Books about it come from the twentieth dynasty of the pharoahs down to twentieth-century America. Analyses of persuasion have been written by some of the worlds greatest thinkers. Many of Platos *Dialogues* were directly concerned either with pointing out the dangers that persuasion can create or with suggesting a system of persuasion that Plato believed would end these dangers. The best-known book, and one of the most erudite on the subject, is Aristotle's *Rhetoric*, a book of enough significance to be included in nearly all lists of "Great Books." The greatest orator of Rome, Cicero, wrote several books about it, as have other statesmen, orators, and philosophers. Others who developed theories about persuasion are St. Augustine, Francis Bacon, and Ralph Waldo Emerson. Two presidents of the United States have taught it: John Quincy Adams was once Boyleston Professor of Rhetoric and Oratory at Harvard, and Lyndon B.

Johnson taught speech before beginning his political career. Nor are other moderns ignorant of the processes of symbols and their influence on mankind. Alfred North Whitehead, Ernst Cassirer, Bertrand Russell, and Susanne Langer are among those outside the immediate discipline who, however, write discerningly about the influence of symbols. Today, we can find analyses of persuasion as prolix as those of Kenneth Burke or as overly simple and pragmatic as those of Dale Carnegie. From this complex wealth of material, we will try to distill principles of persuasion that are indispensable if we are to move our fellow humans in this century.

We need only look into Vance Packard's *The Hidden Persuaders* to realize that persuasion is a source of danger. We can be led to buy things that we do not need, to endorse candidates for public office for irrelevant reasons, and to like and to hate irrationally. Indeed, whenever humanity has been pushed into an unjustified war, persuasion has been one of the potent forces pushing. Persuasion has been used to make the exploited and the tyrannized satisfied with their lot and to condemn those who have had the insight and the goodness to lead us to a better state of existence; it also has served as the tool of the unjustly powerful, the cynically corrupt, and the dangerously ambitious. Why then, should we teach persuasion? By doing so, do we not further impose on humanity?

A naïve moralist might indeed be tempted to spew out a blanket condemnation of persuasion in all its forms. Yet, the evils of removing persuasion (even if it were possible) are greater than those of learning to live with it. There is danger in apathy, and persuasion is one of the mightiest forces for reducing the sterility of apathy. There is danger in inaction, for inaction perpetuates conditions of decay and injustice. There is danger in irrational belief and in taking wrong action, but persuasion can correct our beliefs and our actions. A world without persuasion is one without hope of change. Aside from being a much duller world, a world without the ability to change, refine, overthrow, correct, or reinforce our attitudes, beliefs, values, and behavior would be a world that would make us less human, less free. We would be less in control of our destiny and more at the mercy of the senseless forces that dominate the lives of other animals.

Practically speaking, those opposed to persuasion have no sensible suggestion for abolishing it. Persuasion could be abolished only by boards of censors. Yet censorship is no guarantee of truth: *the best test of truth, Justice Holmes said, is the ability of an idea to survive in the competition of the marketplace. The free competition of ideas is the best guarantee that we will freely arrive at the best answer.* This free competition of ideas implies freedom of persuasion, not censorship of it.

Finally, the best defense against persuasion is to study it so that we can recognize when it is unethically used and when it is used to distort or to stultify or to unjustly dominate. Those who do not study persuasion are apt to have it used against them and to be unable to recognize its use. Therefore, this book aims to present the techniques of persuasion most useful to those among you who would persuade their fellows, and to enable you to recognize the techniques when they are used by others.

Exercises

1. Pericles, the most influential person in Athens' Golden Age, said "Instead of considering discussion as a stumbling block in the way of action, we consider it necessary for any right action at all." Find support for Pericles' idea in ancient or modern history.

2. Could persuasion be abolished? Explain.

3. Besides Justice Holmes' idea that the best test of truth is the ability of an idea to survive in the competition of the marketplace, what are some other tests of truth? What are the tests of truth used in the sciences? In religion? In politics?

4. What are some of the defenses you can use to protect yourself against unethical persuasion?

6
Persuasive Logic: The Tactics of Persuasion

Logic is the basis of persuasion because the normal human being requires, searches for, and responds to a touch with reality. To persuade even the simplest soul to try to jump to the moon would be impossible because the touch with reality of even the simplest soul tells us that we cannot. A logical demonstration can change minds quickly, sometimes easily, and often permanently. Note how logic can change attitudes in the following case.

Most people would avow that the only way to reduce the problem of narcotics addiction is to enforce the law better and to raise the penalties for the possession and sale of narcotics. Yet, northern European countries have used another approach successfully. In those countries, a drug addict is provided, under the most careful medical supervision, precisely enough free narcotics each day to keep him or her from having intolerable withdrawal symptoms. These symptoms drive an addict to steal and even to kill in order to obtain the $75 or more each day that is needed to purchase drugs on the black market. Yet the legal

51

costs of these drugs is only a few cents a day. When an addict is given the minimal dose to prevent the withdrawal symptoms, the addict does not get "high" but is able both to care for his or her own needs and even to hold and perform well certain kinds of jobs. By keeping withdrawal symptoms from occurring, narcotics officials in these countries have abolished the addict's need to commit crimes to obtain drugs, and have ended the mechanism responsible for "pushing" drugs among novices in order to obtain the money to buy one's own drugs. In all of Europe, despite its greater population, the number of dope addicts is only a small fraction of the number in the United States. When it is logically demonstrated that these countries have reduced addiction by this process, so that there are, for example, fewer addicts in all of England than in any one of America's twenty largest cities, many will be persuaded that we have used the wrong solution to the problem of addition.

Facts, figures, examples, testimony of experts, argument from similar circumstances all are persuasive when they have *the ring of reality to them*, because this ring speaks powerfully to normal people. Reason and logic furnish the map by which we can choose intelligently. The development of ability to use persuasive logic is one of the necessary arts required by free men. Let us study its various forms.

The Basic Unit of Persuasive Logic

Persuasive logic has the same basic unit that we described in Chapter 2: the *general statement* and the *support* for the general statement. As before, the properties of these two parts of the unit of persuasive logic are quite different. The general statement "We could reduce the traffic in dope by furnishing addicts with sufficient free narcotics to enable them to avoid withdrawal symptoms" is very different from the facts, analogies, expert testimony, and the like that support the conclusion. Although we will work with the same unit, instead of describing certain *psy-*

chological qualities of the unit of discourse, as we did previously, we will here describe *logical* properties.

Logical Properties of General Statements and Supporting Material

The logical properties of general statements and supporting material are quite different and offer some insights into why logical forms are powerful psychological belief-makers. Let us examine these properties.

General statements, alone, have no logical merit. Supporting material always provides the basis for logical general statements. Let us consider the following general statement; although it will appear to many to be absurd, by supporting material we can give it at least limited logical basis. "We cannot know what the world is like by observing it." The idea seems irrational to the innocently practical, for how else could we know what the world is like? Yet this statement can be given logical merit by supporting it with examples:

> The floor you are sitting on appears reasonably solid. You can test its solidity by stomping on it or by pounding it, and every test you make convinces you of its solidity. But the floor is not solid. It is "made" largely of space. The space, of course, is between the molecules making up the floor, and especially between the electrons and the nucleus of the atoms that compose our "solid" floor. What your senses tell you of the floor is simply not true; neither it nor the earth itself is solid. So full of space are they that someone calculated that if you could take all the space out of all the atoms in the world, you could put the whole world in a wastebasket—if you could find one strong enough. Our senses lie to us about the solid nature of things.
>
> These same senses lie about other things as well. The walls in the room where you are sitting appear to be motionless. But those walls aren't motionless. Aside from rotating about the axis of the earth and revolving about the sun without your being able to perceive it, there is motion inside the walls themselves. Some of the planetary electrons—if we accept Bohr's model of the

atom—are necessarily whirling about the nucleus of the atom at just below the speed of light, and the molecules themselves are in motion. The walls are alive with motion, but your senses do not tell you about it.

Nor do your senses tell you the truth when you see the flashing lights of a railroad signal. The flashing light seems to move, for the same reason motion pictures—which haven't the slightest "real" motion in them (being merely successive *still* frames) —seem to move. Your nervous system adds the "motion," which psychologists describe as the phi phenomenon: the phenomenon of apparent motion. But for all its appearance of reality, there is no motion when we experience these manifestations of phi phenomena. Our senses are again distorting the world.

Our senses tell us that time and space are different things. We would agree that "ten minutes from now" is quite different from "ten miles from here." Yet according to Einstein, time and space cannot be so different as they appear to our senses. We can see that they must be related when we realize that all measures of time are also measures of space: What do the swings of the clock pendulum measure? By swinging through *space*, they measure *time*. Our day is a product of the *space* that any point on the earth must pass to complete one rotation. Our year is the *space* the earth passes through to complete one revolution around the sun. Time and space, which our senses tell us are different are, in some profound way, related. Again, what our senses tell us is not quite right.

The student who is interested in defending the accuracy of the senses will note that we have often used sense data to support the idea that sense data are inaccurate. But, of course, our concern is not with whether the senses give us an accurate picture, but with the logical function of supporting materials. The preceding material reflects the way in which the logical merit of a general statement depends entirely on the kind and amount of supporting material that can be found for it. *The first logical property of the basic unit of discourse is that general statements depend for their truth entirely on the support that can be found for them.* There are some exceptions to this principle: tautologies ("A man is a man") and statements in which the denial of a fact asserts the fact itself ("I do not think that there are such things as thoughts"). The student, however, will not encounter many of these kinds of general statements short of technical courses in philosophy and will not find them of much use in public discussion.

Logic must often come, in point of time, *before* a psychological base can be established. Once we have presented the supporting material for the idea that our senses lie, only then are we in a position to expound the idea in an extralogical manner. We might, having made use of some strongly logical data, clinch our point with the following paragraph:

> The nervous system is like a filter that takes out things that are in the world, like motion, and adds things that are not, like solidity. Our nervous system is a kind of filter, between us and the world, that distorts so that the still frames of a "motion" picture appear to move. The world is no more like what this filter tells us than the music we *hear* is like the sensation we *see* when we look at the printed notes on a sheet of music. Or, if you should have the misfortune to pick up a live wire, you may see "stars," but the stars you see are nothing like the dynamo at the other end of the wire that produced the illusion of stars. Or, as someone else put it, the relationship between the world and the way we perceive it might be like the relationship between the dots and dashes a telegrapher sends along the wire and the meaning they stir up in the person who reads the printed telegram. The real world may be just this different from the world our nervous system shows us.

The analogies used here may clarify the point, may help make it vivid, may clinch the idea so that the audience will remember it, but they must be preceded by logical material or they will only give the impression that you are having trouble with your nervous system. Persuasive logic must often precede the use of psychological materials.

There are, however, certain limitations to the idea that logical materials should precede psychological materials, for the statement is not always correct. Without going inro the complexities of these two kinds of materials (in which we would find that logical materials and psychological materials are far less distinguishable than they appear to a novice), we can conlude by saying that logical materials must precede psychological materials when the purpose of the latter is to *intensify*. Intense feeling is best created only after strong assurance that that feeling is based on a touch with reality. It is no mystery why the powerful crescendos in the speeches of Patrick Henry or Winston Churchill must wait until the logic of the case has been laid before the reader or audience. Logic must often come first.

A third logical property of general statements and supporting material is that *general statements are less reliable than supporting material.* Let us take the following story related by the late Irving Lee in *Language Habits in Human Affairs:*

> A druggist, standing behind his candy counter looked out through the plate glass window and saw, down the street, a man staggering toward his drugstore. As the man approached the store, he bumped into a nearby lamp post, fell down, got up, and wobbled toward the store. He threw open the door, staggered to the candy counter and mumbled something incoherent to the proprietor.
>
> The druggist looked at the man angrily and yelled, "Get out of here, you drunk!"

The imperative statement that the druggist gave reflects an inference that he drew from supporting material: namely, that the man he observed was intoxicated. General statements— inferences—are less reliable than supporting material because *from any incomplete series of data more than one inference can be drawn.* Note the supporting material on which the druggist based his inference: The man wobbled as he walked, bumped into a lamp post, staggered in, and mumbled something incoherent. The druggist arrived at an implicit general statement from this supporting material and, on the basis of that statement, ordered the man out. Yet, as we will see, the druggist had an incomplete series of data, and from it he drew the wrong conclusion. Let us go on with the story:

> Instantly the man straightened up, walked firmly around the candy counter to where the proprietor was standing, grabbed him by the shoulders, and threw him to the floor. Then the stranger calmly reached into the candy counter, took a chocolate bar, unwrapped it, and proceeded to eat the bar.
>
> When he had finished, he smiled at the druggist and said, "I'm sorry to have treated you so severely, but I was suffering from insulin shock. When you called me a 'drunk,' it made me furious, and as you know, anger releases a certain amount of sugar into the blood stream. This sugar made it possible for me to behave

coherently for an instant, and now that I have had a chocolate bar, I am well again. Here's a dime for your trouble, Sir," he said, and walked out while the druggist remained on the floor in astonishment.

We can see immediately that the inference the druggist drew was wrong, but that the supporting material was "right." No one could doubt that the man staggered, and so forth. The inference drawn from this material, however, was unreliable partly because the supporting material was incomplete. Moreover, other inferences just as easily could be drawn from the data given: From the man's behavior, we could infer that he was ill, that he was suffering from a lesion of the cerebellum, or that he was intoxicated. There is nothing in the incomplete series of data to rule out any of these inferences. An incomplete series of data permits one to draw more than one inference; for this reason, general statements tend to be less reliable than supporting material.

But suppose that we did *not* have an incomplete series of data. Suppose that we knew not only the data that the druggist observed, but also such data as how much insulin the man had taken that morning, how much exercise he had had that tended to burn up his blood sugar, how much he had eaten that tended to replace that blood sugar, and especially, what his blood-sugar count was at the time? *As we approach "completeness," only one conclusion can be drawn.* Therefore, the most important characteristic of supporting material is that as we are able to accumulate more and more relevant material, we tend to approach certainty, freedom from error, and accuracy. *Thus, as we accumulate support for our ideas, we tend to guarantee that we are right, that even the most perverse member of our audience will be able to draw only one conclusion from our data, and that our speech will have the ring that a firm touch with reality gives a fine speech.*

We can see from these three characteristics that rhetorical logic is necessarily persuasive for the following reasons:

1. In exposition and persuasion, the logical value of general statements depends entirely on the quality of support that can be found for them.

2. Logical support must come before strong feelings about a subject can be aroused.

3. General statements are less reliable, logically, than supporting material because from any incomplete series of data, more than one conclusion can be drawn; as supporting material reaches completeness, however, fewer and fewer inferences can be drawn from it; and finally, if the support is complete, only one conclusion can be drawn. (Very strictly speaking, we can never have "complete" data because "completeness" entails knowing the habits and values of everyone, which cannot be known, and which, if they were known, would change. In any event, the human being is more than a data processing machine. Nevertheless, for the purposes of a basic course, the more data we have, the fewer mistakes we are likely to make.)

Demonstrating the Logical Strength of an Argument

As a speaker it is your task to demonstrate to an audience that your inferences are warranted—that your supporting material compels assent to your general statements. To demonstrate that your support compels assent requires two kinds of processes: demonstrating the accuracy of supporting material and demonstrating the accuracy of inferences from supporting material.

The Accuracy of Supporting Material
Suppose that you are attempting to show that the national debt is greater than it was in 1945. Because our debt, by the time this book is printed, will have gone from 250 billion dollars to slightly over one trillion dollars, the debt is clearly greater in absolute figures. In such a case, it is easy to demonstrate that your supporting material is accurate. To do so requires that you *cite an*

authoritative source for your statistics. If you have drawn your statistics from *The Statistical Abstract of the United States,* or from any reliable almanac—most of which use *Statistical Abstract* as *their* source—you have done as much as needs to be done to guarantee the accuracy of your supporting material.

If, on the other hand, you argue that severe treatment of juvenile delinquents may increase crime, and you offer examples of delinquents who, after severe punishment, committed worse crimes, the accuracy of your supporting material depends on the accuracy with which the examples were observed and described. Here, again, the accuracy is a function of the *source* of the material. You must be able to demonstrate that whoever observed and reported the delinquents' treatment and subsequent behavior was (1) in a position to know what happened and (2) able to report it objectively. Generally, the accuracy of such observations can be shown in much the same way as with statistical data: by mentioning the observer and by briefly stating the observer's qualifications to observe and report intelligently and honestly. Often the mention of a title that shows that the observer was in a position to know will help qualify the source. If you can, however, you should state the *experiences* the observer has undergone to make that person especially qualified to observe and report. Thus, if the observer is reporting on starvation in India, training that qualified him or her to undertake the study, the time spent at the study, the diversity of areas visited, and the like may all provide the audience with a demonstration that the data produced by the observer were accurate.

Accuracy of supporting material is a function entirely of the source of supporting material. You can demonstrate that the support is accurate by naming and giving the qualifications of the source. Often the source is yourself. In this case, you must, without either pretension or embarrassment, qualify yourself as an accurate observer. This kind of qualification can be done both unobtrusively and effectively. "If you do not think that slums are a problem, I wish you could see the tenement where I grew up, for I was born in one of New York City's worst slums." "Foreign countries *do* appreciate the help the United States gives them. I spent my term in the Peace Corps teaching in Ghana . . . ." "If you think our state governments are more efficient than the federal government, I wish you could have worked with me on the road gang where I spent last summer working for the state. For every man working, there were three to six men watching . . . ." All these statements tend to lend support to the accuracy of the observer's statement, for the accuracy of supporting material can be established by demonstrating that the support has come from a source that observed and reported accurately.

Demonstrating the Accuracy of the Inferences

Although the accuracy of the supporting material is not difficult to establish, to show the accuracy of the inferences drawn from that data is much more difficult. Recall the case of the druggist; he correctly perceived the supporting material: no one could doubt that the man outside his store staggered and wobbled, that he bumped into the lamp post, and that he mumbled incoherently. The supporting material here is absolutely accurate. Yet the inference from this material was wrong. Because accurate supporting material may often lead to inaccurate inferences, we must demonstrate that our inferences are accurate.

There are two ways of demonstrating that our inferences are correctly drawn, and both of them overlap. The first is to demonstrate that no other inferences can be drawn from the data (or that other inferences are either improbably or risky); the second is to demonstrate that the data are complete. How both of these tests work, however, depends on the kind of supporting material used. Let us examine the application of these two tests of the validity of inference on various kinds of supporting material.

The Accuracy of Inferences from Statistics

Suppose you are trying to demonstrate the general statement that our national debt is *smaller* than it was in 1945. The naïve person might think that such a demonstration is an absurdity, because the debt increased from 258 billion dollars in 1945 to one trillion dollars in 1981. But to infer from these statistics that the debt is greater is to draw, perhaps, a wrong inference from the supporting material.

Whether the debt is greater or less is not merely a matter of the absolute figures, but depends on whether the country is wealthier: figures about whether investments, income, and savings have increased or decreased are all relevant. We would likewise need to know whether the private debt, state debts, and city debts have increased, for these also would influence the nation's ability to pay. The point is that the inferences drawn from a statistic must be the result of *completeness* of data; we can see that whether our debt is larger or smaller than in 1945 is not a simple matter and depends on a complete exploration of the amount of debts of various kinds and the amount of wealth of various kinds. Certainly the naïve speaker who things he or she can draw a sound conclusion by merely looking at the debt figures for the 1940s and the 1980s is doing society a disservice in two ways: First, we cannot be sure that the inference from these two figures is correct because the data are more complex, and second a spirit of superficiality is being encouraged by the underlying assumption that such matters are not complex and that a simple "look at the record" will give instant truth. The kind of speaker we need in this century is one who is willing to bring the truth to people, who will struggle to make the complexities clear without undue prolixity, who is logical without oversimplification, and who is persuasive without distortion. Indeed, to so speak is clearly an act of brilliance that deserves admiration and, gratifyingly, often receives its reward.

But it is not only the average citizen or beginning speaker who has been led astray by poorly analyzed statistics; scientists have likewise been misled. Consider the inferences that were drawn from the data of the famous case of "Martin Kallikak." Martin Kallikak—the name is a fictitious one for a real person—was a Revolutionary War soldier who had an illigetimate son by a feeble-minded girl from whom 480 descendants were traced. Of those descendants, only 46 were known to be normal; the other 434 were feeble-minded or prostitutes or alcholics or criminals or a combination of several of these. Kallikak later married a normal girl from a good family; from this union, 496 descendants were traced. Of these, only five seemed to show signs of abnormality, while the remaining 491 were normal, and many were successful in business and eminent in the professions. What inference would you draw from these data? The data are probably accurate, although some questions might be raised about what the observer—who first published the study in 1915—chose to call normal. You might also wonder whether the "better" side of Kallikak's descendants, being more able financially, might not simply be better able to cover up their errors. Still, let us assume the accuracy of these statistics, and ask what inference can be drawn from them. The inference that many social scientists drew from the study was that intelligence and character are hereditary. The "bad" heredity on the illegitimate side of the family produced abnormal descendants, and the "good" heredity on the legitimate side of the family produced normal and productive descendants. Yet this inference is not warranted by the data. The data collector remembered that the abnormal side of the family produced abnormal offspring, but forgot that this side of the family *also had an abnormally bad environment*. Children whose parents are thieves may have "criminal tendencies," not because the children were born that way, but because their environment provided them with knowledge of thievery, with a psychological atmosphere that does not condemn and perhaps rewards thievery, and, especially, with the lack of understanding and lack of appreciation of more legitimate endeavors; the child whose parents are professional people has open doors that the child of a thief or prostitute would never know. Those Kallikak descendants with good heredity *also* had a good environment; and those with bad heredity, a poor one. From these statistics, *no valid inference* about the importance of either hereditary or environment can be drawn.

Certainty, drawing the correct inference is not easy to do, and we cannot formulate rules of certainty that will guarantee accuracy of inferences. The history of science itself is a history of drawing inferences, supporting them, later modifying them, and often eventually overthrowing them. But there is some advice that is important: *Maintain a skeptical attitude, continue to probe, and continue to accumulate information and to search for criticism. Above all, develop a healthy doubt, a questioning attitude toward answers that appear simple.* There are no simple answers—and that statement, itself, being a simple one, is also partly wrong!

The necessity for looking for the *unexpected* in our statistics can be illustrated by an interesting experiment. It once appeared that starvation led to an increase in longevity. In an experiment on rats, those that were fed normally lived 650 days, but those that were denied food one day in every four lived 667 days and those deprived of food every other day lived for 708 days! The simple conclusion seems obvious and inescapable: fasting lengthens life. But, again, the simple conclusion must be viewed with suspicion; soon after these data were published, scientists found that the situation was more complicated than they had originally thought. Indeed, starvation *did* produce an increase in life span, but *only* if the starvation occurred before the rat had reached maturity. Once maturity had been reached, abnormal withholding of food decreased the life span. If you decided that you would lengthen your life by giving up food every other day, you would most likely be wrong. The increase of life span from starvation came about because starvation postponed the development of maturity. A rat does not begin to age until after it has reached a certain point in development—roughly equivalent to the onset of late adolescence in the human being. If we can postpone the arrival of adolesence in the rat, we can increase the rat's span of life. Should we therefore starve our babies? Few would be quick to accept this hypothesis. We do not know whether such starvation would postpone maturity in the human being, or whether the human being, like the rat, can have life lengthened by such a postponement. Moreover, we do not know what might be the effect of such postponement on the energy level, the intelligence, the general health, and the psychological adjustment of either the rat or the human being. It is entirely possible that such starvation, although it may prolong life, reduces the energy level so that although one lives long, one can hardly be said to live well; it is possible that the reduction of nutrition might influence the development of intelligence, and it is quite likely that starvation will not produce a healthy, secure, and productive psychological attitude. Few would care to add a few years to life at the expense of making that life sluggish, insecure, or miserable. Again, the obvious conclusion must be viewed with suspicion. The addition of more information can help correct the obvious.

Let us take one more example to show that the seemingly sound conclusion may be wrong because of an unpredicted and unexpected source of error. Sixty years ago, gerontologists, (scientists who study the causes of aging in people), made the surprising discovery that the length of time people in a given area live was directly proportional to the number of illiterates in the area. At that time, Alabama, which had twelve illiterates per hundred thousand, had ten people per hundred thousand who lived to be over a hundred. Utah, which was the most literate state in the Union, had one illiterate per hundred thousand and had four-tenths of a person per hundred thousand who was a centenarian. Bulgaria, which then had the highest degree of illiteracy in Europe, had sixty-six illiterates per hundred thousand and, correspondingly, had sixty centenarians for the same unit of population. In contrast was New Zealand, which then had the highest literacy rate of any country in the world, having only two illiterates per hundred thousand and one centenarian per hundred thousand. Wherever the study was made, illiteracy seemed to accompany longevity! There were no exceptions.

To some, these figures made sense because illiterates did not know of the burgeoning problems of the world and were not subject to the tensions of someone who could learn the horrors of modern war or the dangerous economic and ecological plight of the world. This conclusion may have been drawn from an ignorant and romanticized view of the illiterate that perceived illiterates as wholesome, natural, vigorous souls not subject to the tensions of other people; the romanticized illiterate was thought to lead a life that was not subject to the competitive terrors of the world of business, politics, and the professions, where the struggle to get ahead brutalizes and ulcerates. But there are too many "jokers" in these statistics. See whether you can find some of them before you read further.

One of the first questions that would occur to the bright mind in exploring whether illiteracy leads to long life is "Is it always the illiterate people who live long?" or the question "Are those who are illiterates and those who live long the *same* people?" From the data as given, we cannot tell. It will occur to the discerning mind that someone who can read might have run across the germ theory of disease and consequently might be more careful about such matters as keeping minor wounds clean and about being sure that his or her food is free from germs and so might avoid certain diseases and live longer. Moreover, the literate makes more money, can afford better medical care, and can reduce the illnesses caused by poor diet, inadequate housing, and insufficient clothing. These matters should lead us to be suspicious of the data. So far there are two difficulties that should occur to the intelligently suspicious: First, are those who are illiterate the same people who live long? Second, when certain aspects of literacy should lead to a longer life, why do we have statistics that seem to indicate the contrary? Yet neither of these, I think, explains the difficulty involved in the statistics. The inference that illiteracy leads to a long life is unwarranted, not because the inference is improperly drawn, but because the statistics are not accurate! At least we cannot *demonstrate* the accuracy of the statistics because in countries where people are illiterate, how do the illiterates, who cannot read and write, *know* how old they are? Among these people accurate birth records are not kept, and the people themselves, being unable to record the date of their birth or count the years that have passed, can hardly give an accurate answer when they are asked, "How old are you?" Again, no precise directions for demonstrating the accuracy of statistics can be given, for there are probably an unpredictable and uncountable number of mistakes that can be made in drawing inferences. The speaker must always be on guard for the unexpected.

Some conclusions follow for the use of statistics: When you base an inference on statistics, demonstrate that you have explored the statistics fully, that you know something about their limitations, about their possibilities for error. For example, it is possible to show that, among college graduates, the C student on the average tends to make less money than does the B student who, in turn, makes less money than the A student. The statistics, along with similar ones, are reasonably convincing. Yet, they should not be presented to an audience without the recognition that there is at lease one possible source of error. The "joker" may be that the fundamental cause of money making may not be good grades, as the figures seem to imply, but that a person who makes good grades *and* who later makes money does both of these because he or she is more perceptive and more intelligent (or, at least, more able to devise ways that result in good grades and more money). Speakers who admit this possibility for error to an audience are, first of all, performing an ethical function in warning audiences of possibilities for error. But the speakers are doing something that is also persuasive: They are showing *that they have been aware of the sources of error, that they have thought about these problems, and that they have arrived at a conclusion as a result of study.* After exploring these possibilities before an audience, the speaker might conclude by saying:

> It may be that good grades and money each come from some independent source such as brains or personality. But if I were a student in school and I knew that I might, by studying furiously for four years, make an additional three hundred thousand dollars in my lifetime (which is the average amount of salary that the A student earns over the C student) I think I would take the chance. If for each year of my four years of study, I could add $75,000 to my income, I would assume that $75,000 a year is very good pay for studying and I would hit the books—and hard.

Such a speaker is no less persuasive than the more simple-minded oaf who simply presents the convincing figures, assuming that the audience is not bright enough to spot errors. A recognition of the complexity of apparently simple matters can give a speech the ring of truth. Speakers who know the most and who can reflect the most crucial and critical aspects of what they know will, in the long run, be the most successful. Other speakers, who use simple-minded tactics, may win an occasional quick battle, but victory in the war will belong to someone else.

The Accuracy of Inferences from Examples

Proof by supporting an idea with examples is the most frequently used of all logical forms; it appears to be the easiest, yet it is often the most difficult to use well. In asserting that fraternities should be abolished because their practices are antidemocratic and anti-intellectual, examples of snobbishness and superficiality engendered by some fraternities are easy to find. But examples of fraternities that have fostered brotherhood and scholarship can also be found. In neither case are the examples cconclusive, except to establish what logicians call a particular premise. A particular premise is a declarative sentence that begins with or implies the word *some.* Thus, the preceding points of view imply that *some* fraternities foster brotherhood and scholarship and *some* do not. Because the premises are particular, no *general* principle about the utility of fraternities is clearly indicated by the data. Because particular premises have severely limited usefullness, many arguments supported by examples are of little logical merit. Our first problem, therefore, is to see how we can use examples in such a way as to lead to a more conclusive argument; later, we will also see that there is a certain value, although a severely limited one, in some kinds of particular premises.

Examples can be used to establish a general statement when the examples are shown to be typical. The following illustration intensified the feeling of distrust many have had of the federal government, yet it clearly misses this necessary test of using demonstrably typical examples:

> A great deal of the taxpayer's money is being wasted on government publications. Senator Styles Bridges once asked all government agencies to send him a copy of their current pub-

lications. Among the more than 83,000 he received were booklets on bats in belfries, how to trap cats, a report on the status of the Cuban frog-leg industry, and a study of North America's fleas.

The four examples cited leave unmentioned the other 82,996 publications; even if the four mentioned were utterly worthless, they would hardly indicate a strongly warranted distrust of government publications. (Even the four might be of significance: Bats, for example, are known to spread hydrophobia; and to the thousands of churches in the United States whose belfries harbor those rodents, the question of how to abolish them might be relevant. The trapping of cats might prevent the present population explosion of strays. Anyone contemplating going into the business of furnishing frog legs for restaurants might find necessary information in a brief pamphlet on the subject, and the habits of fleas would be of interest to chicken farmers and stock raisers, not to mention dog and cat owners.) Therefore, the use of examples in this case is poor, not only because they are not shown to be typical but because the examples themselves may have more utility than one sees from a superficial look at them.

The typicality of an example can be shown in two ways: First, the example can be shown to correspond to the average case. If you argue that teachers' salaries are insufficient to produce the best teaching, you may cite an example of a teacher who must supplement his or her income by summer or other part-time jobs instead of increasing teaching knowledge and skills. You can demonstrate easily that the case is typical by showing that the teacher's income corresponds to the income of large numbers of other teachers. Thus, to show that an example is typical, you must resort to *statistical* data. The example of the low-salaried teacher, when shown to be typical, furnishes that touch with rality that gives rhetorical logic its justly persuasive power. The example shows us the *mechanism* by which low salaries create low endeavor; we see that the activities the teacher must indulge in to earn enough money are contrary to the best interests of education. The statistics ensure that the example furnishes us with a sufficient touch with reality to merit a general conclusion; they are a necessary part of the argument. Therefore, you must find ways of convincing your audience that your examples are not merely isolated bits or extremes that seldom occur; you must bolster your examples with statistical data that indicate that the examples illustrate a general principle.

A second way of establishing a probability that the examples cited are not merely atypical aberrations is to *show that they were selected in such a way that they constitute a fair sample.* Thus, if we wanted to find whether fraternities foster both brotherhood and intellect, we might take a sampling of fraternity members and view their achievements. But if the sample were not carefully selected, the results would be biased. The selection of a fair sample is itself a specialized and intricate technique. We would have to be sure that we had selected a fair cross section of fraternities: we would have to select carefully members not only from several fraternities, but those whose educational background, home environment, college experiences, social experiences, and attitudes are representative. Even professional samplers, such as those who conduct opinion polls, are never quite certain that their sample is as typical as they wish, and they recognize that there is always a certain percentage of error to their predictions. In close presidential races, for example, opinion polls do not give such definitive results that the effect of a last-minute crisis or unusual weather on election day can be overlooked. At any rate, speakers who argue that examples are representative have two choices: they can either show that the examples fit the usual or average case by statistical data, or they can argue that the examples have been selected carefully to include a representative sample. There are no other ways.

But there are some kinds of arguments by example in which it is nonsensical to ask, "Are these examples typical?" Suppose you are arguing that a certain factor is important in the decline of civilizations and you demonstrate that this factor seemed to result in the decline of Roman, Egyptian, and Chinese civilization. It would be nearly absurd to inquire "But are Rome, Egypt, and China typical of civilizations?" So far as we know, there is no such thing as a "typical" civilization. No statistical data and no sampling technique would be of much merit in establishing the idea. In such cases, you must cite *enough* examples to warrant the idea that civilizations fall because of the factor you believe is present.

To take another instance of the idea that examples do not always have to be "typical," some have argued that "Most geniuses are seriously maladjusted." It is doubtful that the idea can be supported by citing a carefully selected sample of "typical geniuses," for, almost by definition, there is no such thing as a typical genius. By their nature, geniuses are atypical, different, variegated, and unique, even *as* geniuses. Therefore, anyone who supports a general statement about the maladjustments of geniuses must examine large enough numbers of geniuses to warrant the generalizations. You cannot use the short-cut techniques of demonstrating that the geniuses fit a general tendency or that they are sampled so that the small sample fits the general pattern. The only recourse you have is to survey nearly all geniuses. (You would of course, find some who were demonstrably well adjusted from many standpoints—Bertrand Russell, George Bernard Shaw, Johann Sebastian Back, Aristotle.) Although it is probably that most geniuses have been maladjusted (at least in somebody's sense of the term), what might be inferred from such a general statement should be viewed with caution. Many infer that such maladjustment is a *cause* of genius. But it is possible that maladjustment is a *result* of genius. To be a genius is to think things that are not known or accepted at present; it means finding answers and even seeing problems that others do not recognize; it means, therefore, that the genius is different from the rest of humanity, which can be, itself, a maladjusting force. Furthermore, the answers found by a genius will not often be recognized and appreciated by others, except after a bitter struggle. Such a situation will merely subject the genius to psychological stress that is conducive to maladjustment. Perhaps being a genius causes maladjustments. We must, again, take care in drawing inferences.

Examples can be used to establish a general principle when they are shown to be numerous enough, although caution must be used to avoid inferring too much from such examples. But what does "numerous enough" mean? If you argue that a given school faculty needs improvement, how many examples do you need to support the idea that "X department lacks competent faculty members?" Or, if you are avowing that "X police force should be reformed," how many examples of bribe-taking officers do you need to support the idea? There is no rule that can apply handily to all cases; again, you must use what Descartes called the "natural light of reason." Rhetorical logic is not a describable science—nor are the principles of science itself completely describable. There is no set of rules that will always everywhere prevent error; therefore, you must always be on the lookout for the unexpected. The best tool that you can develop is a healthy, mature, well-adjusted skepticism to your own ideas. You should be willing to question the probability of your ideas and be willing to admit what improbabilities inhere in them. This admission of possibilities of error will not always defeat your purpose as a speaker, for audiences as well as speakers have within them the natural light of reason and come to respect and trust anyone who admits the possibility of error.

In summary, we have described two ways in which you can use examples to establish a general conclusion: namely, to show that the examples are typical or that they are numerous enough to warrant the conclusion.

There are, in addition, times at which a particular conclusion—one that implies or begins with the word *some*—is useful. Atypical examples or examples that are not numerous enough to warrant a general conclusion are useful to *refute or limit a generally accepted idea*. Sometimes, for example, those of us living in the last half of the twentieth century feel that we have made great progress in perfecting human life—our growth of knowledge, the conquest of disease, the creation of wealth, and the spread of democracy, lead to a vague feeling that "things are better than ever." But when we hear that a woman in New York was stabbed several times by an assailant and that her screams were heard by thirty-eight persons, not one of whom came to her aid, that one example is sufficient to make us wonder whether humanity has improved or retrogressed. Certainly the example assails the general idea that we have made life so grand as the Polyannas would have us believe. Add to the notion more examples of depravity—the murder of both whites and blacks for racial reasons, the number of psychopaths produced by our culture, the vast increase in criminality among the very young—and that our century is the bloodiest in history, and, although we cannot draw any universal conclusion, we *can* cast doubt on the often-accepted conclusion that human life is constantly headed onward and upward. Atypical examples, then, even when they do not support a general principle, can *cast doubt on an already accepted general principle.* Just one example, Karl Popper, the British philosopher, has said in *The Logic of Scientific Discovery*, is sufficient to refute the idea "All crows are black"; all one need do is to find a single albino crow, and the proposition can no longer stand. Particular propositions are especially useful and meaningful when their attempt is to show that something that is *generally* impossible to attain *still may be attainable.* A country, for example, seemingly about to be overwhelmed by a superior power, may recall instances in the past where small armies defeated much greater ones—the examples of Giddeon's four hundred, of Athens with forty thousand men defeating the Persian army of several million, of the American Revolution, the Texas Revolution, and the like, demonstrate that, although small forces generally lose, there have been notable exceptions. Thus, the function of atypical examples is to point out the exception *when the exception is meaningful.* What makes a "meaningful" exception, however, depends so much on the argument and the audience that it is almost impossible to describe. Yet we can hazard an attempt: *The exceptional example and the atypical case can be used meaningfully when they force an opponent or an audience to modify a previously universal and unsophisticated general statement.* An argument in which one person avows an idea and his or her opponent avows the opposite, and each has supporting examples is often ineffective. For example, if you insist that fraternities encourage intellectual development and cite examples of fraternities that invite stimulating speakers to the fraternity house, expend money on books for the library of the house, and enforce study hours, and your opponent cites fraternities that encourage inane and childish activities at all hours of the day and night, that overemphasize the social and sponsor "wild" parties, you are both supporting unintelligent conclusions. The idea that fraternities (implying "all fraternities") do one or the other is untenable. The more sophisticated speaker will permit the exceptions that his or her opponent might bring to modify the conclusion so that it becomes "Fraternities that are concerned with the intellect of their members find ways to stimulate it." This conclusion is more sophisticated and more accurate than the usual ones supported in discussions. *Thus, examples that cannot support a general conclusion still may force an intelligent modification of a general conclusion. This intelligent use of the exception to modify a previously universal and unsophisticated conclusion is largely responsible for growth in the sciences. The exception forces a modification in the process of generalizing and in that way performs a stimulating service.* Examples and instances can be useful both in supporting or refuting general statements and in forcing modifications of those statements.

The Accuracy of Inferences from Analogies

The analogy, as we have said, is a special kind of example for arguing that what was true in a previous situation may be true in the present one. If, for example, you are arguing that the honor system reduces dishonesty at the University of Virginia—where the system has long been in practice—you may legitimately argue that it will reduce cheating in a similar university. If Greece declined because she failed to solve the problems of war and poverty, you might argue that if we fail to solve these problems, we may decline, as well. Thus, *the analogy is argument based on similarity.* Of course there are never in human history two cases that are identical, and for this reason, analogy is not thought well of by logicians. No other university is exactly like the University of Virginia, and no other civilization was ever like Greece; therefore, conclusions drawn from these cases are far from certain. But *nearly all* conclusions in the realm of public discussion are far from certain. Public discussion is concerned with uncertainty. Technical logicians, on the other hand, usually do not carefully inquire into forms of reasoning that yield other than absolutely certain conclusions. Logicians, although with less frequency than in the past, are concerned with grounds for certain and undoubtable belief; hence, they often have failed to say much that illumines reasoning in human affairs and in public discussion. The strength with which they condemn the analogy is hardly understandable, for it is no weaker—and no stronger—than other forms of support. The example, as we have seen, can be, has been, and will be used both stupidly and mistakenly; the same is true of statistics, testimony, and any other form of support. But the analogy *is* worthwhile, for it makes available to us the experience of similar situations. Without using it, each nation, each city, each person for that matter, would have to begin afresh. If northern Europe has solved the problem of illegal drug traffic, and if analogies were as worthless as some would have us believe, Europe's experience would not indicate to us the slightest possibility of how we can solve the same problem. If the way in which malaria has been wiped out in North America has no meaning—has no analogical significance—we would not be so successful in destroying the same disease in southern Italy and South America. We know, contrary to the prevailing notion of some logicians, that similar circumstances can teach us *much.* The problem is not to avoid the use of the analogy, but to learn to use it intelligently. Let us suggest some ways the analogy may be a useful logical tool in discourse.

If you use an analogy, you are under an obligation to perform two functions: *you must show that the idea you wanted accepted was true in the analogous case.* Thus, you must show that Greece actually *did* defeat an army much larger than her own or that cheating *is not* a problem at the University of Virginia or that the traffic in drugs *is* almost nonexistent in northern Europe. *You must be as careful and as painstaking as the case requires to demonstrate that the idea was true or worked elsewhere.* To use the case of the sharp reduction in drug traffic in northern Europe, you must give the figures on the sale of illicit drugs now and what they were in the past; if the figures are not available, (and, perhaps even if they *are*) you may want to give the figures for the number of arrests of addicts now as opposed to previously. (In the latter, you might also want to quote reliable police authorities that the reduction in arrests in Europe for addiction is not due to any lack of desire to enforce the law, but is the result of a general reduction in the number of addicts.) When you have used examples, statistics, and testimony to thoroughly demonstrate that the idea was true or worked elsewhere, and when you have discussed—as an intelligent person should and usually will—the limitations of the truth or workability of the idea, then you may want to undertake the second burden in using analogies.

You must show that the cases in which the idea was true or worked are similar in all significant respects to the present situation. Thus, the intelligent speaker will note that northern Europe offers no particular political organization, no attitude of mind, no social condition that would explain its success in limiting drug traffic. You should show that there is no explanation for the reduction in drug traffic except that northern European governments give narcotics in limited amounts to addicts; by keeping addicts from experiencing withdrawal symptoms, Europeans have reduced the motivation of the addict to sell dope to obtain money for the purchase of black-market drugs. Or you must show, to take another case, that there is nothing at the University of Virginia—not the southern code of honor, not any aristocratic or democratic attitude, not any special education in Virginia secondary schools—that accounts for the success of the honor system in reducing cheating. The University of Virginia, in all essential respects (save one[1]) is like most other universities; the differences between it and other schools would not be such as to account for the success of the honor system. For the analogy to be useful, the situations must be shown to be analogous. Among beginning speakers, too few take time to demonstrate the analogous relation between the situation in which their idea was true or worked and the situation in which they are trying to persuade an audience that it again will be true or work.

Whether situations are analogous is not always an easy matter to decide. Sometimes basically analogous situations are found in circumstances that differ markedly. We might usefully argue that it may, one day, be possible for earth to have some kind of beneficial world government, and do so on the basis of an analogy. Of course, there never has been a world government, but we might honestly argue that the United States provides a valid parallel. Especially would this be true if the audience felt that the differences in the world are too great for us to ever agree on a single government—even if it were conceded that such a government offers strong possibilities for preventing nuclear war. We could argue that the differences among people in the United States before 1787 were nearly as great as the vast diversities present among the world's peoples today. What did the erudite, educated Bostonians—some of whom had the best education the world offered—have in common with the frontiersmen's unlettered but instinctive "woods-wisdom?" What, indeed, did the Indian have in common with the New York shipper? How could one ever reconcile the vast differences between the frugal, hard working Puritan and the wealthy, slave-holding Virginia cavalier? Two states had already declared war on each other, but were unable to fight it because the state between the two refused to permit armies to march over it. The United States had within it the Yankee ship captain, the slave, the soldier, the merchant, the sharecropper, the one who spoke no English, the

---

[1] The University of Virginia *does* have one significant difference between it and universities that do not have the honor system: it has a *long tradition* of the honor system that has worked. We must not presume that universities can build a successful tradition overnight, and they probably cannot without a long and wisely prepared orientation period.

foreigner—of which millions more were about to come—all of whom represented differences in styles of life, in codes of living and in economic desires and demands. Yet we formed one government from the many.

Although this analogy can be debated, it has merit. And often the most sophisticated speakers will be able to draw their greatest wisdom from analogies that at first glance are far-fetched, but that, upon closer analysis, turn out to be relevant. The unsophisticated speaker, until he or she becomes familiar with analogical thinking, generally should restrict himself or herself to the closest possible parallels. Yet all speakers should be on the alert for significant parallels in situations that differ widely in their more superficial aspects.

There is one noteworthy exception to the idea that we must always show that the two situations being talked about are similar. Suppose, for example, you were supporting the idea that superhighways with a median strip separating those going in opposite directions are safer than those without such a strip, you could support the idea by giving figures from highways that cut through cities, those from country areas, those from the plains states, and those in mountainous areas. In so doing, you would be supporting the idea that the median strip contributes to safety *regardless* of the conditions. You would not need to show that the cases reviewed were similar to those in which a median strip was recommended. To take another example, better street lighting seems to reduce crime, wehther the lights are installed in a crime-prone slum, a suburban area, or a rural area. Hence, the usual analogical necessity of demonstrating that these conditions are like the one in which the speaker is recommending street lighting are irrelevant and even nonsensical. Therefore, whenever a speaker can show that an idea is true or has worked in a great diversity of circumstances it may be unnecessary to show the similarity between these circumstances and the particular situation in which he or she recommends that the workable idea be applied.

Analogies make available to us the experience of other persons and places. Analogies can be dangerous kinds of evidence to use, because mistakes can be made with them; however, they are no more dangerous than any other kind of support. When they are used to show that an idea was true or worked in similar situations, they are as reliable as any other tool available to the speaker.

The Accuracy of Inferences from Testimony

Much of the material you use comes from other sources. You must rely on someone else to discover the average income of inhabitants of the Appalachian Mountain area, the effects of smoking on the lungs, or the current profits of the small farmer. Unless you have performed expert studies on the matter about which you are speaking, you will have to rely on authoritative publications, specialists, and fact-finding commissions. Many of your statistics, examples, analogies, and even general statements will come to you from other sources, so that much of your speech will be built from testimony. Let us see how testimony can be used with some sophistication.

QUALIFYING EXPERTS.   If you quote Frank Lloyd Wright, who said "An honest arrogance is infinitely preferable to an insincere humility," there is not much point in carefully qualifying Wright as an "expert." Certain kinds of testimony stand by themselves and are not, strictly speaking, instances of the use of an expert who is qualified because of the careful and extensive studies he or she has performed. The pithy saying, the *bon mot*, the sharply phrased slogan, do not draw their appeal from the expertise of their creator; rather, these forms symbolize an idea that is perhaps already vaguely felt by the audience—the forms are accepted because they appropriately and vividly express that idea. To be sure, acceptance of the epithet often is enhanced psychologically if the author is well thought of by the audience; we are not less apt to accept the idea that "No problem facing mankind is beyond the reach of human beings" when we find that it was written by John F. Kennedy. But the powerful expression of a general statement by a prestigious person, although often an aid to persuasion, is not a logical matter and need not concern us here, except to enter a brief disclaimer by mentioning that it would be inappropriate to qualify authorities in such cases.

But much of the use of testimony requires that we carefully qualify the agent giving the testimony, because the truth of the conclusion depends almost entirely on the expert's expertise. When, for example, we quote Robert M. Hutchins to the effect that "It is possible to make bombs of such size that two of them could wipe out all life in North America," whether Mr. Hutchins knows what he is talking about becomes crucial. We would not be helped if we knew that for nearly a decade he was America's youngest college president, nor would he be qualified because he had stimulated much thought and many changes in under-graduate education at his own university. Nor would it be of the slightest merit that he has worked with the Fund for Adult Education of the Ford Foundation. But if we knew that he was Chancellor of the University of Chicago at the time of the Man-hattan Project—which created the first atomic-fission bomb—and that, as Chancellor he was necessarily the principal liaison officer between the physicists working on the project and the federal government, and for this reason *had* to know the nature of the project and the possibilities inherent in atomic fission, we would begin to see that he might be qualified. Thus, the problem in the use of testimony is to demonstrate that the testimony was given by an agent who is in a position to know about the matters on which he or she is testifying. *Experimental inquiries have shown that the message being conveyed to the audience will be accepted in proportion to the credibility of the source.* An audience generally accepts the testimony of a credible source, and the acceptance of that testimony is in proportion to the perceived value of the source. Because this is so, speakers can increase the audience acceptance of an idea if they can increase the belief in the authority testifying about the idea.

There are many ways of helping an audience realize that testimony is being given by a qualified expert; and, depending on how important it is that the audience be impressed with the expert's qualifications, one or more of these ways should be used: You can explain that the agent giving the testimony has performed a careful study on the matter involved. The person who has spent years in empirical or experimental work on the effects of tobacco smoke draws authority *from* that experience, and the speaker quoting such an authority should tell the audience about the time the expert has spent and the kinds of studies he or she has made. Too often, inexperienced speakers let an expert's qualifications depend only on the mention of a title, saying, "Dr. B. is director of experimental research at such-and-such institution." The use of such a title may enhance the expert's prestige and many times may be sufficient to have the audience accept him or her as an expert; but if the authority's qualifications are crucial, there is no substitute for explaining both the training and experience the authority has had in the matter on which he or she is quoted. In addition, the prestige of the person quoted may be better understood by the audience when the opinion of other experts in the same or closely related fields is given. The general opinion of the expert held by other experts in the same field is often crucial, although such opinions are difficult for the speaker, who may be untutored in that field, to find. Yet if you can discover the reputation of an expert among other experts in the same area, you can further convey the expertise of that person to an audience. The agent's special studies, publications, titles, reputation, and honors won all may lead an audience to believe in what the expert says; depending on the doubt that an audience may have either in the agent giving the testimony or in the testimony itself, these means of qualifying experts should occupy a significant place in the speech.

Not only should the agent giving testimony be a person who has undergone experiences that make him or her especially knowledgable, but sometimes it will be necessary to show that the expert is not influenced by undue bias. Be suspicious of the testimony of presidents on the value of their administrations because of the not remote possibilities for bias. In general, the speaker should eschew those sources that may be accused of bias. However, avoidance of those who might be biased is too facile a solution to the problem. There is hardly anyone whose expertise has led him or her to new insights who has not been accused, by someone, of bias, mistakes, omissions, and the like. Particularly on matters that are currently controversial, we find that those who are experts are charged with ineptness, error, and prejudice and that they often countercharge that other experts in their field who represent different points of view have other biasing tendencies. There is no easy solution to the problem. The speaker, as always, must use the natural light of reason, must weigh authorities with care, and must select those who have both carefully and objectively studied the matter on which they are quoted.

Testimony is no more unreliable than statistics, examples, or analogies; yet it may be wise to be somewhat more suspicious of the "expert" than we often are. After all, who *is* an expert is extremely difficult to determine. Moreover, experts, *particularly in times of intellectual crisis*, are often wrong. At the time of Galileo, nearly all the experts were wrong, and only Galileo was right. The entire medical profession, with the single exception of the English physician, Dr. Lister, was wrong about the cause of disease, and only Louis Pasteur was correct when he taught that organisms so small that they could not be seen without a microscope could bring the strongest person to weakness and death. Sigmund Freud was condemned and reviled by the experts of his time and the list doesn't end with Freud. Whenever the world is on the verge of new discoveries, those who have a vested interest in avoiding or minimizing the new discoveries may resist them. Fortunately, the spirit of science is such that, with increasing frequency, new discoveries are accepted instead of resisted. Albert Einstein and Niels Bohr did not die of persecution—their discoveries were incorporated into physics with an encouraging immediacy that catapulted them to fame while they were still young. But outside the sciences, conditions have not much changed in the last thousand years. Sigmund Freud's greatest influence came after his death; the major economic principles of John Maynard Keynes were not applied in the United States until after he was dead. We must suspect that there will be other cases in which most of the experts will be wrong, and the one who is ignored, maligned, and forgotten may be right. Great ideas start out with a minority of one.

For psychological reasons, we should be cautious of the overuse of testimony, because much testimony consists of general statements. As we have seen, "We need a better Pure Food and Drug Law" is a general statement and it is not particularly interesting to an audience. Nor is the attention value of this general statement much enhanced if we say, "The chairman of the Federal Trade Commission testified before Congress that we need a better Pure Food and Drug Law." General statements, whether they stand alone or are made by an expert, still possess certain undesirable characteristics. We should, therefore, plan to support expert general statements with concrete supporting material, if for no reason than that support will make the idea more interesting.

But there is an important logical reason for being cautious of overusing general statements, even when they are the distilled thought of a careful and intelligent authority. Recognize that testimony is often a *secondary* logical source. That is, it often involves the *conclusion* of a person or an investigating body, and conclusions, as we have seen, are subject to error. When possible, we can avoid some inaccuracies if we ask for the *evidence for and reasons for* the conclusion rather than just the conclusion. The primary matters are the evidence and reasons that have led the expert to the conclusion. We should be wary of blindly accepting an opinion without making an attempt to inquire into the evidence for the opinion. This evidence provides the logical strength of the expert's opinion, and where we can locate and understand the evidence, it is logically better that we present *it*, instead of only the general conclusion the expert may have formed.

Be skeptical of testimony. Yet it is unavoidable, for we all must make use of other sources. And be skeptical about experts, for experts have often been wrong. Nor is it easy, always, to discriminate the sound expert from the unsound expert. As with all forms of evidence in human affairs, we must use our head, search for the unexpected, and look for possible errors. Yet testimony is no weaker a form of support than any of the others we have discussed. It can and often must be used; moreover, it can be used intelligently. Because we must borrow ideas and facts from others, we must strive to use with maximum skill materials that come from other sources.

On the Nature of Rhetorical Logic

Because of the elementary nature of this book, the discussion of rhetorical logic has been restricted to a description of the uses of statistics, examples, analogies, and testimony. Because the normal human being requires and responds to a touch with reality, and because these logical forms can furnish that touch, they persuade audiences. In looking back on these forms, we can see that rhetorical logic is nearly always a demand for *evidence*.[2] If someone insists, for example, that government aid to education will result in government control of education, evidence must be presented: the *testimony* of experts in political science and education and *analogies* of similar situations in which governments have "helped" an institution and, by so doing, controlled it. Anyone with the opposing views, believing that federal aid will not necessarily mean federal control, likewise must present evidence: he or she can give the *example* of the GI Bill of Rights, through which several billion dollars were given for educational purposes without federal control of schools or school systems occurring. Thus, *rhetorical logic is largely a function of the use of supporting material or tactics.* There are some exceptions to this idea, and were this text more advanced, we would describe

[2] Rhetorical logic is often considered to involve, as well, the study of deductive inference; however, such study is out of place in an introductory text in persuasion because of its involved nature. Little can be done with deductive logic in less than an entire semester. But more important, the demand for logic in the discussion of human affairs *is* a demand for evidence. Propositions are supported by evidence and refuted by evidence, and seldom indeed do the constructs and fallacies of deductive logic play a part in public discussion. Therefore, a consideration of deductive logic is omitted here, because the application of it would play only a minor part in the activities of either the intelligent speaker or the intelligent listener.

them; for the most part, however, rhetorical logic can be equated with tactics.

As will be seen in the next chapter, these logical tactics can be used to support strategy that results in emotional appeal and motivation; emotion and logic are not separate, but can work together. The base of a strongly persuasive speech, however, lies in the logical tactics used; when these tactics are wed to psychologically designed strategy, the speech, because it is a powerful union of a strong touch with reality and a touch also with that which spurs human beings, will be as effective as the case permits.

Exercises

1. Think of five times in your life that supporting material—evidence—changed the way you thought or felt. Describe each case, and explain why you changed. In retrospect, was the change warranted? Explain.

2. Although political candidates are not noted for extensive or careful use of facts, statistics, or examples, who among them, in your opinion, makes at least some use of these materials? Support, from your examination of such a candidate, the idea that the candidate uses support well.

3. Because listeners do not demand extensive and careful use of supporting material, candidates do not use such material well. Devise a plan by which at least the younger generation could be educated to expect and demand of their candidates that good supporting material be used.

4. Who among present office holders and candidates makes especially poor use of supporting material—too little support, or support that may be inaccurate or that leads to inaccurate inferences?

5. Choose two people in history who used supporting material very well and two who used it poorly. Demonstrate that the two who used it well did so, and that the two who used it poorly did so. Explain in each case wherein the merit or lack of merit existed. Be sure to support your contention from the speeches or writings of each person.

6. Prepare a casebook of the accurate use of supporting material and the accurate drawing of inferences from it. Explain why each case is a good example of the use of logical materials.

7

Emotion and Motivation: The Strategy of Persuasion*

PEOPLE OFTEN SAY that they buy food freezers because a freezer will enable them to save money. Saving money is usually an admirable urge, generally considered the most rational of desires. In buying a freezer to save money, however, one is still following an *urge*, however admirable, or a *desire*, however rational. In other words, one is following an emotion and is buying because of motivation.[1] Emotion and motivation are the movers.

---

*This material was first published in *The Quarterly Journal of Speech* XL:(Oct. 1955) 271-278. It has been modified for use here.

[1] Forty years of studying emotion and motivation and thirty years of teaching courses in rhetoric and motivation have not convinced this writer that there are separate drives, or that distinctions, although possible, between the terms "emotion," "motivation," "drive," "urge," "feeling," "want," "desire," "wish" and the like are rhetorically useful. For rhetorical purposes, these terms may be used synonymously. If the traditional motivational terms are not useful, useful statements, can be made about attitudes. Such an idea does not sound exciting, but wait until you see how it works. See Cullen Bryant Owens, "A Survey of Social Psychology as Bearing on the Teaching of Speech," unpublished Ph. D. thesis, Cornell University, Ithaca, N. Y., 1946. The dissertation, regretably, is little known; however, it is sound, worth knowing, and by no means out of date.

Rather than being bought to save money, it is more likely that freezers are bought for reasons that are less sensible—reasons that touch on one's strong, but less intellectually acceptable, feelings and motives, as Vance Packard tells us in *The Hidden Persuaders*:

> Economically, the freezers didn't make sense when you added up the initial cost, the monthly cost added on the electric bill, and the amount of frozen leftovers in the box that eventually would be thrown out. When all the factors were added, the food that was consumed from the freezer became very costly indeed.
>
> The freezer represents to many the assurance that there is always food in the house, and food in the home represents security, warmth, and safety. People who feel insecure . . . need more food around than they can eat.[2]

Although freezers are often sold because they represent security, even when they are sold for the most admirable of reasons, that reason seems to be rooted in emotion and motivation. Things and—it is well to remember—ideas are "sold" because they gratify deep-seated feelings or needs. Sometimes the needs gratified are irrational. But regardless of whether the "selling" is rational or not, no one can be led to buy a thing or an idea unless there is some appeal to feelings, needs, drives, desires, wants, emotions and motives, all of which, for our purposes, are words that are synonyms—although with slightly different connotations that make one of the terms sometimes more useful than the others. But let us abandon the sales metaphor, because what is true of sales is not always true of other kinds of persuasion. We do not so much "sell" ideas as we connect ideas with our motives—by, for example, showing that a certain idea will fulfill a need. Without the need, we will not accept the idea; just as the adage says, "You can lead a horse to water, but you can't make it drink." Also, Samuel Johnson observed, "You cannot convince a man against his will." What you want another to do or believe will not be accepted unless it appeals to that person's *needs*. To persuade, we must appeal to emotion and motivation, and the best supporting material must support ideas that evince motives.

[2] New York: Pocket Books, Inc., 1958, pp. 61-62.

Ethics and Psychological Appeals

Is it ethical to appeal to one's emotions? Sometimes emotions drive one to do things that are not wise. On the usually accepted assumption that anger was wrong, or at least that anger made one behave ineffectively, Thomas Jefferson advised, "When angry, count ten before you speak; if very angry, a hundred," and the advice is generally good; follow it, if excessive anger discombobulates you. Benjamin Franklin observed that "What'er's begun in anger, ends in shame." Even stronger is Horace's insistence that "Anger is momentary insanity." Even love, some say, distorts: Francis Bacon insisted that it was impossible to love and at the same time to be wise. (One is inclined to say, "So much the worse for wisdom," but the problem of the ways in which emotions are held to distort thought and cause dangerous reactions doesn't go away.) Someone once said, "I know love is better than murder, because love makes two people happy, and murder only one." But perhaps all emotions are bad; in *As You Like It*, Shakespeare says that love is merely a madness; Alexander Pope damned all emotions by saying, "What reason weaves, by passion is undone." If these emotions are so dangerous and evil, then we should not teach people to arouse them. We must ask, "Are appeals based on emotion and motivation necessarily wrong, mistaken, immoral, or distorted?"

Emotion and its cohorts have long had a bad reputation. Plato banished poets from his Republic because they evinced emotions and emotions distort reality. The Greeks, by more than this adage, recommended reason: "He that will not reason is a bigot, he that cannot reason is a fool, and he that dares not reason is a slave." Not to reason is to be less than human. The coming of the Age of Reason, in about the eighteenth century, gave further impetus to the idea that emotion was wrong: it seemed to increase the power of religion, to give dangerous power to mobs, and to help preserve such notions as the divine right of kings. More recently, Freud and those influenced by him have found that emotions are often unconscious in origin, beyond the gentle control of reason, and hence are especially dangerous. Emotions are used by propagandists, warmongers, agitators, and racists. In the face of such charges, how can we dare to teach others to use emotion and motivation?

Let us assume, at least for a moment, that the charges against the use of emotion and motivation are correct—or, at least, that we want to avoid emotion and be able to quell it wherever it arises. To do so means that we cannot escape understanding how to produce an emotion, because, rationally enough, the opposite of the way that produces an emotion is the way to quell it. For example, if we are angry with our neighbor because we think that we have been harmed, the anger may be reduced or eliminated if we are shown that we have not been harmed or that whatever harm we suffered was caused by someone other than our neighbor or that if the harm was caused by our neighbor, it was unintentional and the neighbor is willing to more than recompense us for our trouble. To be able to discover such ideas for the reduction or removal of emotion means that we must have the same information and the same techniques we would need to whip up an emotion. Because we need knowledge about emotions if we are going to reduce an emotion or if we are going to produce it, that knowledge will be conveyed in this book.

But let us look at the assumption that emotion is necessarily bad. Is emotion, as such always—or usually—evil, unintelligent, or subhuman? In an article now become a classic, the psychologist, Ronald Leeper pointed out that when we condemn emotion and its cohorts, we do so on the basis of what emotions in their extremes drive one to do.[3]

If emotion in its extremes is disruptive of reasonable behavior, and therefore should always be avoided, then so should breathing, for if you breath too much and too rapidly, you will faint from hyperventilation. We do not discover the function of any chemical by judging what it would do to us in gigantic doses. For example, salt, water, and iodine are each necessary in some amount to all human beings, but each if overused can be a

---

[3] "A Motivational Theory of Emotion to Replace 'Emotion' as a Disorganized Response," *Psychological Review* 55:14 (1948). The entire article is worth studying for the serious student of ethics and emotion.

poison. In a like manner, we should not use what happens when extremes are present as indicative of normal psychological processes. In mild amounts, fear can be beneficial: Edmund Burke said, "Early and provident fear is the mother of safety." Some emotions are admittedly good, at least usually. Few people would care to live without confidence or joy. Burke, again, said, "Next to love, sympathy is the divinest passion of the human heart." Anger can unify a people to halt the injustice of certain abuses and improve the condition of humanity. True, anger in its extremes can destroy intelligent combat in a fighter or reduce an otherwise sensible human being to seeming idiocy, but so can almost any desirable reaction in extremes. Leeper's point, that we must not judge emotions in extremes anymore than we would judge other matters, is a sound one. He adds that animals, above the level of the oyster in the evolutionary scale, when disturbed respond to danger in time to save themselves, are more apt to desire to care for their young, and are more likely to survive. He calls for the development of emotional richness as well as the development of the "brainy side of life." Indeed, total lack of emotion is not a sign of intelligent behavior; however, it is a certain sign of death. The emotionally unresponsive person is not an ideal, as Dorothy Parker is said to have observed of someone she disliked: "She ran the whole gamut of her emotions, from A to B." Because emotion is not inherently bad, because emotion can contribute to creativity, to humane action, and to survival, and because emotion adds intellectual richness to our experiences, we should understand, develop, and control it, rather than avoid and ignore it.

The psychologist Abraham H. Maslow points out that emotion and logic are not opposed in the healthiest persons, and each may contribute to the other, at least in people who have reached the most desirable state of development. Only in the neurotic—one who is at odds with him- or herself—does reason struggle with emotions.[4] It is important to add that because intelligence is based in the *subject* of a speech, and emotion is

[4] *Motivation and Personality,* (New York: Harper & Row, Publishers, 1947), p. 233.

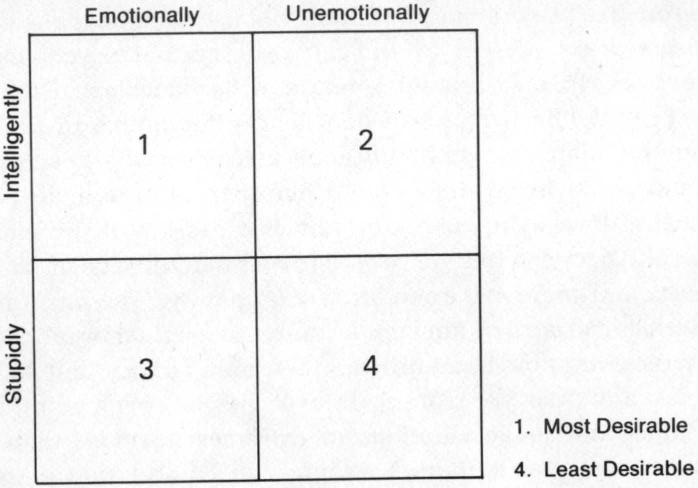

FIGURE 1. This figure is adapted from a diagram produced by the late Irving Lee, Professor of Speech, Northwestern University, whose courses, increased my interest in the study of motivation and emotion.

based on *feelings in the audience*, intelligence and emotion can mix in various ways: We can behave emotionally and stupidly (as some unthinking worshippers of the Age of Reason insist is characteristic of all emotional thought and behavior), but a better response is to behave emotionally and intelligently (see Figure 1). Psychologists have found that motivation, provided it is not too intense, can increase our ability to learn, can contribute to our creativity, and can increase our ability to solve puzzles and problems. We can, as Figure 1 suggests, behave unemotionally *and* unintelligently. The ideal is the opposite: to behave intelligently and emotionally and thus reap the rich rewards in energy, persistence, and variety that emotion can bring to intellectual matters.

Difficulties with Our System of Analyzing Emotion and Motivation

Generally when motivation is treated in books of rhetoric, a list of "motives" is given. "Sex," "self-advancement," "loyalty," and the like are alleged to be motives. Of course, no two lists of motives, whether by psychologists or rhetoricians, are the same; that one list is correct and the others wrong seems improbable. But even the most exhaustive list of motives together with discussions of the nature of each motive furnishes the student of rhetoric with only an imcomplete analysis of the process of motivation. Such motives as the "desire for security" may be looked on as *generalized goals* toward which the organism moves. The generalized goal of security may be gratified by securing a better job. Thus, motivation, as generally treated in rhetoric, hardly involves more than a consideration of certain kinds of general and specific goals. Yet the process of motivation is more complex than a movement toward goals. For example, what is the effect on motivation of a goal from which we are restrained by a barrier? It will be shown later in this chapter that such a situation significantly conditions the problem of persuasion. What implications are there for persuasion when we attempt to appeal to a motive and the process of gratifying that motive subjects us to danger or the possible loss of other goals? What are the implications for persuasion when goals, motives, or desires are in conflict? Most treatments of motivation ignore these significant and complicating variations. Furthermore, attitudes, sentiments, stereotypes, and opinions, although related to motivation, are commonly treated as separate entities. It is possible, however, to integrate them into a theory of motivation. If motive situations involve barriers, threats, conflicting attitudes, sentiments, stereotypes, and opinions, how do these matters change what Aristotle called "the available means of persuasion"? Certainly no mere list of motives, however long, can make clear all the possibilities and implications of these problems to the student of rhetoric. The simple situation in which the individual is motivated toward a goal is by no means the only situation in which motivation operates. We need a doctrine of motivation that will utilize these complicating features of motivation.

It may be possible, paradoxically enough, that the study of motivation would be advanced if we, temporarily at least, abandoned the search for motives. We could describe motivational *situations* in which the human being behaves. The contemporary rhetorician, Kenneth Burke, offers a suggestion. He says that the concept of "motive" is nothing but a shorthand term for a situation. Burke is well known for finding five situations whose totality includes every aspect of rhetoric.[5] But we seek situations that will include only aspects of motivation rather than the totality of rhetoric. Let us see what all aspects of motivation have in common.

The Nature of Emotion and Motivation

When we experience an emotion or become motivated, exactly what do we experience? What is emotion and motivation from the standpoint of the one who experiences these states? To experience emotion and motivation is simply to be *involved. Persuasion by emotion and motivation is persuasion by showing or suggesting that the listener is self-involved.* When we are out of town and happen to read in our hometown newspaper an account of a fire that devastated one of the homes in the town, we may experience some emotion—much more than we would reading about a fire in another town. If we find that it is our own home that has burned, the emotion intensifies proportionally to the involvement. Self-involvement is a necessary basis for emotion and motivation. So universal is self-involvement as a basis of human life that Nietzsche observed that those who, by not talking about themselves, suggest that they are not interested in themselves have only a very refined form of hypocrisy. So basic to human life is self-involvement that Schopenhauer insisted that if we were not so excessively interested in ourselves, life would be so dull that none of us could endure it. To be involved in a situation means precisely that powerful emotions and strong

[5] Kenneth Burke, *A Grammar of Motives.* (New York: George Braziller, Inc., 1955), part I.

motives are aroused. Persuasion by emotion and motivation, therefore, is the process of *involving* other people in ideas.

But it is not only persuasion that requires self-involvement; exposition also does. "Teach your daughters about the diameters of the planets," said Samuel Johnson, "and wonder when you have done why they do not delight in your company." We must adapt to the interests, which is to say, *to the involvements* of our listeners. Good speaking, whether expository or persuasive, requires that an audience be led to feel involved. Let us inquire into the rhetorical means for achieving this involvement.

The Rhetoric of Emotion and Motivation

Ethics and Rhetorical Structure

Emotion and motivation are matters of strategy—ideas, general statements, points—that, if believed strongly enough, will elicit feelings of self-involvement. We get angry if we believe that "So-and-so has taken what belonged to us and has done so intentionally." But if nothing is taken from us, or what was taken was in no way valued by us, or the person taking it did not realize it was ours, we are not involved. It is clear that emotion and motivation are the result of carefully chosen general statements leading to self-involvement and the support needed to make those general statements clear, reasonable, and vivid. With this understanding of the rhetorical nature of emotion and motivation, let us take a closer look at the ethics of emotional and motivational appeals. Because emotional appeals are matters of rhetorical strategy, the rightness or wrongness, the rationality or irrationality of the strategy are functions, in part, of whether strong logical support can be brought to ideas. Emotional appeal and motivation, therefore, are not necessarily disorganizing, irrational, unbalancing, tricky, or dishonest. Suppose you find an idea that can elicit an emotional response, and suppose you support this idea with strong and valid statistics, with intelligently chosen examples, and with a barrage of carefully selected expert testimony. In this case, you would have aroused an emotional response or motivated a person by powerfully supporting a psychologically oriented idea with logical materials. You might, for example, say to a friend, "Smoking three packs of cigarettes a day, as you do, is likely to cause cancer"; if you support the idea extensively with excellent logical materials, your friend will feel involved. Many who were not motivated to stop smoking before careful scientific evidence was compiled demonstrating the relationship between smoking and lung cancer did stop when strong logical materials showed them that smoking can lead to an early and painful death. Thus, psychological appeals and logical materials are neither opposites nor mutually contradictory. Logic is a function of supporting material and evidence, and the psychological appeals to the emotions and motives are functions of strategy. The two can be used in conjunction with each other so that a unit of discourse that involves them both can be at once psychologically compelling and logically convincing. Every unit of discourse consists, as we have seen, of two parts: an idea and the support of the idea. *The soundest forms of persuasion involve the selection of an idea in which the listener is involved—one that arouses emotions or motives—and the support of that idea with the strongest possible logical materials.* This kind of persuasion energizes people but does not do so in the style of the demagogue, of the charlatan, of the spellbinder. It is at once logical *and* powerful. That emotion-producing ideas and ideas that motivate can be both sound and ethical is no new discovery. It is implicit in the work of Aristotle who, throughout his *Rhetoric*, suggested hundreds of kinds of ideas that could change perceptions and would cause people to act. We will attempt to organize and systemize these kinds of strategy so that you can select from them the kinds that are strongest and most relevant for each case.

Ideas—strategy—when supported by strong logical materials, can lead others to a perception of self-involvement. When perceptions of self-involvement occur, they seem to occur in five basic kinds of situations. A situation in which we face an un-diagnosed difficulty, in which we are oriented toward a goal, in which we are prevented from seeking a goal by a barrier, in which we are subject to one or more threats, and finally, in which we are identified with the welfare of others.[6] Let us examine the lines of argument that can be taken in each of these situations.

The Undiagnosed Difficulty Situation

The difficulty situation is one in which the subject knows that something is wrong but doesn't know exactly what. John Dewey stated that no one ever thinks unless he or she is confronted with a "felt difficulty."[7] His discovery was perhaps the most impor-tant contribution to the understanding of the thought process in history. We do not think about our feet until the shoe pinches. *Difficulty* begins thought, not easy living, as so many had thought. But undiagnosed difficulties are more important than even Dewey thought. Freud pointed out that even such appar-ently unmotivated actions as slips of the tongue, mistakes in typing, and dreams come about as a result of undiagnosed, perhaps even unrecognized, frustrations.[8] The first motivational situation is one in which members of the audience feel, vaguely or precisely, that something is wrong, without knowing exactly what. It could be something they ate, something they exper-ienced (maybe lack of sleep). Anyway, they don't feel right but have no idea why, to take one kind of example. The person who has a dull pain in the stomach may not know the cause of the difficulty but may simply know that he or she feels poorly, without being able to locate the anatomical region where the problem is centered. The difficulty may be as vaguely defined as

----

[6] The article from which this chapter is adapted appeared in 1955 and has been anthologized several times. Because no one has yet to suggest that there are more motivational situations than the five suggested originally, these may be all-in-clusive of motivational situations.

[7] *How We Think.* (New York: D. C. Heath Co., 1910), p. 9.

[8] Sigmund Freud, "The Psychopathology of Everyday Life," in *The Basic Writings of Sigmund Freud*, A.A. Brill, trans. (New York: Modern Library, 1938), pp. 35–181.

"the mess in Washington," or may be as hidden as the neurotic's complaints.

Let us explore some of the rhetorical implications of this motivational situation. "Rhetorical implications," here mean the possible lines of argument a speaker may take with an audience that is, or can be put, in this situation. The implications given here for each of the five situations are only suggestive of the vast number of possibilities that might occur. Here are a few of the rhetorical possibilities:[9]

1. Deny that there is a difficulty; belittle the importance of the difficulty; point out that yielding to the difficulty is unworthy, or point out that others in similar situations paid no heed to the difficulty.[10]

2. Help the audience to realize the importance and the pressing nature of the difficulty as something deserving or requiring its attention.

3. Locate and define the difficulty; urge the audience to define the difficulty and locate the causes of the problem, or set up procedures by which such diagnoses could be evolved and such causes located.

---

[9] Those acquainted with the *Rhetoric* of Aristotle are aware of his *topoi:* a *topos* is a general idea capable of being supported with specific materials. In Book II of the *Rhetoric*, especially in Chapters 2–11 (1378a–1388b) he lists those kinds of strategy that can evoke anger, confidence, fear, indignation, pity, and the like. But many of the chapters in Book I can also be said to be motivational, for they suggest *goals* toward which the audience can strive: happiness, the good, the noble. Clearly, however, he had—although he never explicitly stated it—the idea that emotion could be evoked by a general idea that could be supported by intensely logical materials. Many of the arguments over the dangers and disorganizing tendency of psychological appeals would have been avoided had Aristotle's view been understood: that emotions came from an *idea* that was capable of logical support. Far from bifurcating logic and emotion, he welded them together, so that the same arguement is at once both psychologically and logically compelling. Aristotle, however had a clear egoistical bias, of which he was apparently unaware, but that must be overcome. See Don Burks, "Psychological Egoism and the Rhetorical Tradition," *Speech Monographs*, XXXII: 400–418 (Nov. 1966).

[10] Because each of the kinds of strategy is capable of considerable modification and extension, this possibility of varying the strategies will be suggested to the student if, after each statement, he will read "and so forth." Human beings, with their infinite variability, cannot be described by even this rather lengthy list of psychological strategies. In no sense is the list complete and final.

4. Attack a particular formulation of the difficulty as irrational, unjust, unworthy, and unworkable.
5. Direct attention to other difficulties on the grounds that they are more significant, more pressing, more open to solution.

The Goal Situation

A typical and familiar motivational or emotional situation is one in which the audience desires a certain goal. When the audience is in this situation, there are a number of kinds of strategy that you can use:

1. To urge the audience to achieve a goal, you can support some of the following ideas:
   a. The goal can produce benefits for the audience: wealth, pleasure, happiness, security, prestige, freedom, or growth. (Why do we never find people laboring to convince us that we would be happy if rich?)
   b. The goal is among the most significant or important goals the audience can seek. (You must attain some sophistication, however, about what truly is significant, important, worthy, good. It is best to remember the caution of Emerson: "The virtues of society are the vices of a saint.")
   c. The goal is deserved by the audience; it may be taken by those less in need or less deserving unless the audience responds quickly. (Curiously, do not most people believe that they deserve the good things of life?)
   d. The goal is easily attainable by the audience. (Ease of attaining a goal may often encourage an audience to seek it; on this basis, Mussolini led the Italians into the misbegotten war in Ethiopia and the Russians attempted to conquer Finland. Nevertheless, one of

the most effective appeals in history was Winston Churchill's promise that all he could bring to England, as she seemed to be dying, was "blood, toil, sweat, and tears." Normal people are often persuaded by what is difficult, sometimes partly because it is difficult. There are, of course, abnormal people who have an appetite for grief and pain, so that sometimes the opposite of the idea is persuasive.

e. The goal is necessary for the audience's survival. (How could a few thousand Greeks turn back a Persian army numbering from two and a half to five million? They probably could not have, had their survival not required it.)

f. The goal will bring benefits to, or is deserved by, or is needed by those with whom the audience is identified: family, friends, those in the same occupational group.

g. The goal will bring long-lasting or permanent benefits to the audience. ("Therefore, whosoever heareth these sayings of mine, and doeth them, I will liken unto a wise man, which built his house upon a rock; and the rain descended, and the floods came and the winds blew, and beat upon the house; and it fell not: for it was founded upon a rock.")

h. Lesser men do not seek the goal, but only those who are superior. (Nietzsche observed that we never dive into the water to save a drowning man more eagerly than when there are *others present who dare not take the risk*.)

2. To urge the audience to give up a certain goal, support some of the following ideas:

a. The desire for the goal is unworthy of the audience; to seek it is irrational, unjust, and contemptible; admirable people in the same situation have not been tempted by it. ("O.K. So my suit isn't in the latest style. What do you want me to be—a fashion plate?")

b. The goal is unnecessary and would not meet a

significant or worthy need or would not be long last-
ing. (Most arguments that contain the words "Who
cares . . . ?" are expressions of this idea.)

c. Other goals are more pressing, more possible to attain, more satisfying, more permanent. ("Lay not up
for yourselves treasures upon earth, where moth and
rust doth corrupt and where thieves break through
and steal; But lay up for yourselves treasures in
heaven, where neither moth nor rust doth corrupt,
and where thieves do not break through nor steal.")

d. The goal would be injurious, rather than helpful or
pleasant, or would produce benefits of a question
able nature, or is not what it appears to be. (This
topos is exemplified by the "sour grapes" approach.)

e. Use the opposite of some of the kinds of strategy in
the preceding section.

The Barrier Situation

*The strategy available to a speaker changes when a barrier is
interposed between an audience and the goal it seeks.* Some obvious barrier situations follow: To a small child, the goal may be
a piece of candy and the barrier the glass case. To the college
student, the goal may be a good grade and the barrier the
amount of work required to obtain the grade. Such situations are
extremely common. No student becomes a lawyer without years
of study, no runner a champion without patience and effort, no
person a good cook without long trial and error. In a sense, we
are always separated from our goals, except at the instant of
achieving them, by the barrier of time.

The barrier situation is one that develops or reduces anger,
which when intense enough can become hatred. Should we ever
hate? Christian tradition urges us to "turn the other cheek," and
surely some turning would have prevented more than a few
murders and a few wars. "Hate is prolonged anger," says the
adage, and is best kept under control. Yet is all hate bad? Should

we not have hated Hitler, and did not our hate shorten World War II as well as insure its decisiveness? Buddha asked, "If we reward evil with kindness, with what will we reward good?" Perhaps even hate is not always, bad. When people need to be united, Checkov observed, "Love, friendship, respect do not unite people as much as a common hatred." But suppose that anger is out-of-bounds? We can allay anger by taking the opposite position of the following ideas. Anger seems to thrive when repression is used. William Blake's "A Poison Tree" is worth thinking about:

> I was angry with my friend:
> I told my wrath, my wrath did end.
> I was angry with my foe:
> I told it not, my wrath did grow.

Expressed anger is apt to evaporate, especially if the cause of the anger is removed.

Finally, on the ethics of anger and hatred, Aristotle observed in the Nichomachean Ethics, "Anyone can become angry—that is easy, but to be angry with the right person, to the right degree, at the right time, for the right purpose, and in the right way—these matters are not easy."

More speaking is done in the context of a barrier situation than in any other. The lines of strategy from which you can choose in such a situation are different from those in the goal situation:

1. To urge the audience to try to achieve the goal, despite the barrier, use the following kinds of strategy:
   a. Increase the desire to get through, over, or around the barrier by increasing the desire for the goal. (See the first group in the goal situation.)
   b. The barrier is contemptible, unintelligent, unnecessary, or unjust. (Recall how you felt about unnecessary but difficult "busywork" assigned by a teacher.)
   c. The barrier works to the advantage of the enemies of the audience.
   d. The agent that raised the barrier is contemptible,

unintelligent, or unjust. (The Declaration of Independence said of George III: "He has called together legislative bodies at places unusual, uncomfortable, and distant . . . for the sole purpose of fatiguing them into compliance with his measures.")

e. The agent that raised the barrier has treated us with indifference or disparagement. ("Men may forgive injuries, but none ever forgive contempt.")

f. The agent that raised the barrier has given to others what the audience deserves. (Remember how you have felt when something you have believed *you* deserved was given to *another*.)

g. The agent that raised the barrier acts as if he or she were doing the members of the audience a favor, or has tried to make them feel shameful when they have not deserved to feel so. (Often the stereotype of the "do-gooder" suggests the preceding reaction, or the parent who says "You must eat your spinach before you can have ice cream because spinach is good for you.")

h. The agent that raised the barrier has injured or treated with indifference or disparagement those with whom we identify ourselves: family, friends, home, country, occupational group.

i. The agent that raised the barrier has slighted us, or those with whom we are identified, in regard to our strongest virtues.

j. The agent that raised the barrier has received good treatment at our hands, but has not returned it, or has returned less than he or she received, and has done so deliberately. (How do we feel about those countries we have helped but which then become neutral or even hostile to us?)

2. To urge the audience that the barrier should not be surmounted:

a. The barrier is a necessary one, or was instituted because of our own wish for it, or was raised inadvertently by some act of our own, or those who raised it did so for our own good, or did not intend to cause us harm. ("Every luxury must be paid for twice: once when you buy it, and then when you suffer the hangover it produces.")

b. The *opposite* of any of the ideas that tend to make an audience crash through or go over the barrier may tend to make them believe that the effort may not be worth it. (See number 1 under barrier situation and the members under 1.)

c. Any strategy that tends to weaken the desire for the goal will also weaken the audience's desire to surmount the barrier. (Use the opposite of 1 under the goal situation.)

d. Request that the audience study the barrier and goal more carefully. (Keen understanding comes only after careful study, yet many a power figure realizes "To kill an idea, appoint a committee to study it.")

The Threat Situation

Still different kinds of strategy are available to a speaker who faces a threat situation. In the previous situation, a barrier is imposed between the individual and a goal; the barrier, although perhaps detestable, is relatively inactive because it can only prevent us from attaining a certain goal. In the threat situation, we may subject already achieved goals as well as future ones to loss; the threat situation produces fear.

It needs to be emphasized that fear is not an emotion to be employed lightly. Strong emotions can turn against us. "Short is the road from fear to hate," runs the adage. One should note that Caesar became a victim of fear, all the more because he understood the possibility that fear could backfire, for he said, "He must necessarily fear many whom many fear." Be certain that arousing any emotion is justified; but when you are sure, go ahead. The following possibilities are suggestive:

1. To urge the audience to resist and combat the threat, use the following lines of argument:

    a. The threat has the power to harm the audience if it is not responded to promptly and powerfully. ("The greatest problem could have been solved when it was small." Patrick Henry is supposed to have said, "But when will we be stronger? Will it be when we are totally disarmed, and when a British guard will be stationed in every house?")

    b. Great effort can reduce the threat and has done so under similar circumstances. (It was also Patrick Henry who said, "We are not weak if we make proper use of those means which the God of nature has placed in our power. Three millions of people, armed in the holy cause of liberty, and in such a country as that which we possess, are invincible by any force which our enemy can send against us.")

    c. Justice, morality, or the good life demands that the threat be combatted. ("The loss of liberty to a generous mind," said Alexander Hamilton, "is worse than death.")

    d. The audience possesses sufficient courage, power, and intelligence to resist the force. (Again from Patrick Henry: "The battle is not to the strong alone; it is to the vigilant, the active, the brave.")

    e. Others less able than the audience have combatted similar forces courageously and successfully. (Take care, however, not to produce strong feelings of shame, for they are generally not conducive to high achievement, which requires more confidence than shame.)

    f. The means, help, ideas, techniques (and the like) for combating the threat are at hand or will inevitably arrive. (In concluding his speech on the disaster at Dunkirk, Churchill said, "And even if . . . this island or a large part of it were subjugated and starving, then our Empire beyond the seas, armed and guarded by the British fleet, would carry on the struggle, until, in God's good time, the New World, with all its power and might, steps forth to the rescue and liberation of the old."

2. To urge the members of the audience that the threat may overcome them, use some of the following lines of strategy:

   a. The threat, which will harm or destroy the audience, is superior to the audience's power to resist and is close at hand. (Before World War II, Frenchmen were so demoralized by the belief that Hitler's troops were invincible that they capitulated readily.

   b. The threat can harm or destroy those with whom the audience is identified: family, friends, colleagues.

   c. Others, who are similar to the audience, have been defeated by the force before, although, perhaps, they did not expect to be.

   d. Help is far away; the audience is alone without allies, resources, or the strength to resist. (Robert Ingersoll said, "We cry aloud, and the only answer is the echo of our wailing cry.")

   e. The weaknesses, rather than the strengths, of the audience have been attacked.

   f. What the force attacks is not worth keeping, or would be injurious, or could not be enjoyed if kept. ("He who fights and runs away lives to fight another day.")

   g. Good sense requires that we give up the goal, or men of honor have given up in the face of similar forces. ("Let us, like the British Empire lose every battle—except the last one.")

The Identification Situation

The last of the motivational situations is one in which human beings become involved because they identify themselves with others. When we identify with a person or group, their problems become our problems, their struggles are our own, and their failures and successes are experienced as if they had happened to us.

1. To urge the audience to identify itself with another person or group, use the following strategic ideas; use them together:

   a. The person or group is in need—is facing difficulties not of its own making or not its own fault—and that we, were we so threatened, would consider formidable. (Sympathy is not felt for those whom we consider better off than ourselves.)

   b. The person or group is like us in background, purpose, attitudes, ways of facing life, education, status, hopes, plights, and even in mistakes made. (We do not identify with the ant someone crushes on the pavement—unless we endow the ant with human characteristics and see the ant as one who experiences hope and pain as we do. To feel sympathy for an individual or group, we must see similar aims, hopes, feelings, and fears. Even showing that we make the same mistakes may be a tie!)

2. To urge the audience not to identify with a person or group, use these ideas:

   a. Some individuals in the group represent values, attitudes, hopes, aims, and ways of life that are hostile or strange to other members present. (Appellations like "nigger," "wop," and "kike" emphasize nothing of the common humanity that minorities share with majorities.)

   b. The need the individual or members of the group face is not a great one, has been exaggerated by them, is their own fault, or they are able to solve it alone.

   c. Granting them aid at this time would expose the

audience to danger, would be largely wasted, and is unnecessary.

The preceding possibilities are sufficient to suggest a wide range of kinds of strategy that are available for a speaker to use with audiences in various situations. These ideas for strategy can be modified to fit the particular subject, and they are capable of many variations; sometimes two or more of them work especially well together, so that the use of one reinforces the use of the other. At any rate, you can see the kinds of ideas that tend to involve the audience in a situation and that, therefore, tend to arouse emotions and motives.

Strategy in Emotional and Motivational Arguments

The preceding strategies are only half the strategies implied in this chapter. Each one has its opposite, which can be used. Thus, the amount of variety open to speakers is enormous. Select the best strategy to suit the audience, using whatever guides you have to what would fit the audience, and whatever hunches experience has given you. The ideas should be appropriate to you as well as to the audience. A devout Christian, for example, may not wish to arouse anger but may search for situations and ideas that fit his or her particular religious commitments. Find out what kinds of ideas are inappropriate for you. In addition to fitting the audience and the speaker, ideas must suit the occasion. Some occasions require solemnity, some require humor, and some require other moods. Choose ideas that, if they do not perfectly suit the occasion, at least do not do violence to the occasion—unless that is your deliberate intent. Finally, the speaker's subject must be included in the matters the speaker should consider in selecting ideas to evoke an emotional response. Some subjects lend themselves to some of the situations and ideas more clearly; war lends itself to anger, hatred, and fear. Peace lends itself to joy, hope, and fulfillment. Each subject has certain ideas that are more natural or more compatible to it. Find ideas that best suit the subject, yourself, the audience, and the occasion.

Tactics in Emotional and Motivational Arguments

The strongest speeches, it must be re-emphasized, are not those that utilize a large number of emotional and motivational ideas. These ideas are general statements, and even though they are potentially emotion producing and motive arousing, still, when they stand alone, without the use of supporting material, they are dull, sometimes unclear, and lacking in demonstrable validity. *The psychologically strategic ideas we have outlined here derive their strength from the supporting material the speaker furnishes.* It is even more important in psychological arguments to limit the number of general statements—that is, to limit the number of psychologically strategic ideas—and to support those selected with the best tactics possible. Distilling the subject down to a few crucial general statements that fit the audience, the subject, the occasion, and you, in the best possible way, is an absolutely necessary art. Simply because you are using ideas that can stir up emotions and motives you may not assume that you need not limit these to the fewest and best. Because the strength of these psychological ideas depends on their support, limit the number of general statements as carefully as in exposition, where you use more neutral ideas.

Again, select from the kinds of ideas suggested in this chapter those that are most apt to arouse an emotion in the members of the audience and to motivate them—those most likely to make the audience feel involved. These ideas, as in exposition, should be few in number, clearly and vividly stated, selected so as to suit the particular audience, and chosen or phrased so that the points are related to each other. Above all, *the points selected must be strongly supported.* Before constructing your first persuasive speech, review the suggestions for choosing ideas in Chapter 4 and for supporting ideas in Chapter 3. These chapters apply to the support of emotional and motivational ideas as well as to expository, or logical, ideas.

Exercises

1. Recall a time when you were very angry. What caused your anger? Can you locate one or more of the ideas under the barrier situation that were responsible? What might have placated your anger? How could you have done so?

2. Repeat the preceding exercise for each of the five situations presented in this chapter: recall a time when you were, clearly, in each of one of the five situations; try to determine the cause; if you moved out of the situation, what helped you to do so?

3. Recall one or more times you were justifiably angry. What made the anger justifiable? Do the same for a time when you were afraid. What made it justifiable for you to be afriad?

4. Find examples in advertising that exploit emotions. Analyze the techniques being used. Do the same for a candidate running for office: What did the candidate do that made you believe exploitation was used? How can the exploitation be combatted?

5. Find examples in your life of times when you felt an emotion—when you were motivated by feelings that added zest or strength or helped you think better. Show that you were better for having had the emotion or feeling.

8

The Ethos of
the Speaker

ALEXANDER THE GREAT'S army was never larger than forty thousand men, and usually it was half as large, but it followed Alexander for ten years, away from the comforts of home, surrounded by danger, across deserts, over mountains, and through swamps, conquering mighty cities and whole empires. What held the men together? A large part of the reason that they stayed with Alexander was that he had unique authority, leadership, ability, charisma, prestige, or in a word, *ethos*. What the men in his army thought of him made them believe and follow him, risking their lives, undergoing privation and even facing death. When, however, the army began to think less of him, as when he seemed to adopt more and more the manner of an oriental despot and to claim that he was a god, they revolted and refused to go farther. The most powerful means of persua sion may be one's self; when that self seems admirable and, conversely, when that self seems less than admirable, it may impede our ability to persuade. As Emerson observed, "What you are speaks so loud I cannot hear what you say." How we are perceived by an audience is a powerful persuasive force. We may define this force, our ethos, as *the image of the speaker, or as the way an audience perceives a speaker.*

If what an audience thinks of a speaker is so important a means of persuasion, we would expect that when the members of an audience perceive a speaker as being worthy or admirable they would be persuaded by the speaker, but if the members of an audience perceive the speaker as being other than admirable, they would not be persuaded. To demonstrate experimentally that such is the case is easy. In the first experimental attempt to see how differing perceptions of a speaker—differing kinds of ethos—influenced attitude change, three audiences—equated in age, sex, and other variables—listened to a recorded speech in which socialized medicine was favored. The audiences were similar, but one audience was told that the speaker was the Surgeon General of the United States, another audience was told that the speaker was the Secretary-General of the Communist Party in the United States, and the third audience was told the speaker was a sophomore college student. Each audience was tested before hearing the speech and after hearing it, to see what kind of shift in attitude would occur, if any. The speech supposedly given by the surgeon general changed the attitudes of the audience significantly in favor of socialized medicine, whereas the speech by the supposed Communist and the sophomore did not.[1] Our perception of the nature of the person speaking to us changes our perception of the speech. We perceive the work of those with a favorable ethos as being good, whereas the work of those with a poor ethos is perceived as poor. *The nature of the agent performing an act changes our evaluation of the act and changes its influence on us.*

Just so, the ethos of a writer seems to influence our evaluation of his or her writing. In an experimental attempt to study the nature of the agent in communication, students were asked to rank passages written by sixteen different authors.[2] A month

[1] Franklyn S. Haiman, "An Experimental Study of the Effects of Ethos in Public Speaking," *Speech Monographs* XVI:190–202 (Sept. 1949).

[2] Muzafer Sherif, "An Experimental Study of Stereotypes," *Journal of Abnormal and Social Psychology* XXIX:371–375 (Jan.–Mar. 1935).

later, these same students were asked to rate a different set of passages, each attributed to the same sixteen authors but actually all written by Robert Louis Stevenson. Three-fourths of the students reflected the same attitude they had in the first experiment. That is, if the passage were attributed to Joseph Conrad and a student gave the passage by Conrad a low rating in the first experiment, that student also tended to rank low the passage attributed to Conrad in the second. This experiment reflects, again, the importance of the image of the agent in communication. If we think a painting was done by Leonardo da Vinci, we are apt to think well of it, just as we are apt to trust what we read in what we consider a reliable newspaper, to believe what we hear from a person whom we consider to have prestige, and to be influenced by someone we consider to be a statesman. Aristotle recognized the persuasive power of ethos over two thousand years ago and believed that it was "almost the most important means of persuasion." [3] His analysis of the nature of ethos is still worth studying.

Aristotle on Ethos

The kind of ethos that makes one persuasive, Aristotle theorized, comes from three indispensable qualities: intelligence, moral character, and good will. Let us look at all three.

Intelligence

We are not persuaded by someone who seems stupid. Consider your own teachers. If you were asked to list the two or three best teachers you have had, probably not one of them seems to you to be unintelligent. Consider the most effective speakers in the past—philosophic speakers such as Socrates; religious speakers such as Moses, Jesus, and Gandhi; political speakers such as Pericles, Lincoln, or Churchill. No speaker considered "great" by the members of an audience was also considered by them to be

[3] Rhys Roberts, trans., *The Rhetoric of Aristotle*. (New York: Modern Library), 1954, p. 25 *1356a*.

stupid. Churchill's wartime speeches were considered great and intelligent, but his postwar speeches, particularly those on economics, are thought to be, to put it kindly, uninformed; his wartime ethos helped hold Britian together, whereas his postwar ethos got him tossed out of office. Insofar as a person has ethos, he or she has it only, according to Aristotle, when that person is perceived to be intelligent or wise.

Character

The second quality that constitutes ethos, according to Aristotle, is moral character, but not in the negative sense of the term—that is, as being Victorian. Moral character is the ability and willingness to do things for others. Just as we are not persuaded by one who appears to be stupid, neither are we persuaded by one who appears to be a self-seeking, or a selfish and dishonest speaker. The popularity of Richard Nixon when he was elected by the largest majority in American history slipped just as he was about to be impeached, and people who previously would have believed almost anything he said were no longer willing to follow him.

Good Will

Finally, Aristotle insisted, one cannot develop strong ethos unless one also has goodwill toward the audience. If we perceive that a person dislikes us, we will not willingly follow that person. Perhaps you have liked another and then found out that that person disliked you; thereafter that person's influence over you probably disintegrated.

To have moral character in Aristotle's sense—that is, to wish good things for others—and good will seems to be related; if you have one, you should also have the other. Yet consider the parent who says to the child, "Eat your spinach or you cannot have desert." The statement undoubtedly reflects a desire for the child to follow a good diet, to avoid sweets until enough nutrients have been eaten. Yet the statement, and the tone of voice in which it was probably delivered, resulted in a threat. Moral character is not always the same as good will, and you can have moral character without good will.

Evaluation of Aristotle's Concept of Ethos

By and large, Aristotle's analysis was a brilliant one, and for two thousand years the best discussion of rhetoric.[4] But it presents certain difficulties. It is true that if an audience thinks we *lack* intelligence, character or good will, we will not be persuasive. And it is true that we ought to believe those who have these three qualities, and that we, more often than not, do believe them. But we do not always accept those who seem intelligent, who seem to be of good moral character, and who seem to have good will. Consider the "celebrity": whoever the current film or television stars, idols, or "personalities" are, their popularity is rarely explained by their fans' perception of their intelligence. Nor is the fainting of spectators, their screaming, or tearing off the clothes of their idol explained by the idol's transcendentally splendid moral character, or by the idol's great good will for humanity. Aristotle's trinity cannot explain the prestige of many of these celebrities, whose styles of life, dress, and hairdo are cherished and imitated. Something is wrong.

Modern Analyses of Ethos

If there is something wrong with Aristotle's analysis of ethos, modern analyses have done little to overcome the difficulty, which, for the most part is itself unnoticed among professionals. In modern rhetoric the list of qualities has been expanded from three to many, adding some Victorian virtues such as sincerity

[4] For a more thorough analysis of Aristotle's concept of ethos, see Otis M. Walter, *Speaking Intelligently: Communication for Problem Solving* (New York: Macmillan Publishing Co.), 1976. Ch. 7.

and miscellaneous and quasi-Freudian qualities such as sex appeal, vitality, virility, femininity, and pleasing appearance. Yet mere lists do not account for people's worship of celebrities, powerful political figures, or great religious leaders. Let us look at the difficulties with such lists.

Atoms vs. Patterns

Both ancient and modern descriptions of ethos are based on the assumption—an assumption that may have blocked the thinking of rhetoricians since the time of Aristotle—that we can understand ethos when we know the parts of which it is constructed. Because there has been little new analysis of ethos in the past two thousand years, this assumption may be blocking thought. The kind of assumption that states that we can understand the whole when we understand its parts is called an atomistic assumption. Atomism searches for elements; atomism has, at times in the past, been used successfully. Joseph Priestly, who, in addition to being a world-famous chemist was also a rhetorician, discovered oxygen and found that it was necessary for life. When he was followed by Cavendish and Lavoisier, who found and described the function of other parts of air, it appeared that atomism was *the* way to understand things. The idea that one way to understand things was to analyze their elements was distorted to "The *only* way we can understand things is to find their elements," or as you may have heard it in school, "You can't understand a thing until you know its parts." But we cannot understand engines by looking for their elements. Even though we know all the elements of which an engine is made—iron, carbon, copper, aluminum, molybdenum, and the like—such knowledge does not tell us how engines work. Strikingly different engines are made from the same elements: a water pump is different from a lawn mower, and yet each can be created out of exactly the *same* chemical elements. On the other hand, identical engines can be cast from different chemical elements: an excellent automobile engine may be case from iron or aluminum. (We can argue that iron, aluminum, copper, and the like are not the functional elements of engines and that the carburetor, pistons, and crankshaft are. But then, if determining the elements is as ambiguous and uncertain as this situation suggests, of what use here is the concept of elements?) If the same chemical elements can produce different engines and different elements can produce nearly identical engines, then an understanding of elements of which an engine is made will not give us much understanding of engines.

If we do not look for elements, then we must look for patterns. The difference among engines made of the same elements lies in their patterns: the lawn mower and the water pump may be made of the same elements, but they are cast in different patterns, and these patterns account for the differences. If engines made from different elements (at least iron or aluminum) are cast in the same patterns, they will be similar in function and power. Patterns help us to understand ethos, as well.

Patterns of Ethos Based on Need

When we examine the ethos of people who had powerful ethos, we find that it seems to be based on needs of the audience, and those needs furnish the keystone to a pattern of ethos. No one, for example, can account for the ethos of Adolph Hitler among Germans from 1933–1945 without understanding the needs Germans felt. They were faced with defeat and desperation and thus were vulnerable to one who posed as their savior, as the one who would deliver them from disgrace, unemployment, and poverty to glory. Note that Hitler's ethos in the 1930s was perceived quite differently by most Americans, whose needs were different, and who considered him, therefore, differently; Americans perceived him as a lunatic. In Germany today, where needs are different from what they were in Hitler's time, Germans are both incredulous and embarrassed by the adulation accorded Hitler decades ago—except for a small minority, perhaps a lunatic fringe, whose needs are different. Hitler's way was paved by the poverty brought by defeat and the Great Depression, leading people to welcome one who in better times they would have ignored or ridiculed. Thus, Hitler's ethos was perceived differently:

> What people are willing to believe is not simply a matter of the credibility or legitimacy of the ideas, rules, and persons offered them. It is also a matter of their own need to believe. What they want from an authority is as important as what the authority has to offer.[5]

Needs furnish the organizing principle by which we construct the image of the speaker. Let us examine some of the patterns of ethos, each of which will have a different set of needs, and each of which will be successful or unsuccessful depending on the needs the audience feels.

Glory Figure Ethos

Alexander, Julius Caesar, Mohammed, Hitler, and Churchill all had one characteristic in common: what can be called glory figure ethos. Each of these resembles what the psychiatrist Eric Fromm has called "father figures." However, because women can have the same kind of ethos—consider Joan of Arc for example—the name *father figure* is inappropriate. The ethos of such persons arises because of the desire of audiences to escape the pain and responsibility of making choices. To realize that we are free to make choices, but that there is no universally recognized way of making the best choice (and that even the word *best* is so ambiguous that some have called it a meaningless word), and that religion may guide some people, selfishness still others, and one or more philosophies may guide others is painful. Nowhere can we find the guide that is recognized by all as the correct, infallible guide. The possibility of making the wrong choice on the road where at nearly every instant we are presented with forks (alternatives), some of which are surely better than others and others of which may lead to destruction, is a

---

[5] Richard Sennett, *Authority.* (New York: Alfred A. Knopf), 1980, p. 25.

prospect that many people find a form of torture. However, by finding a person who is "right" and following that person, it may appear that we can escape the pain and responsibility of making choices. The glory figure is one who is perceived as making the right choices, and to follow such a figure is to automatically be "right." Such figures are often, especially when dimmed by being from the distant past, imbued with miraculous abilities: We have mentioned the "miracle" of Alexander leading a tiny army to attack the most powerful empire in the world. We should also note that the teen-ager Joan was able to lead armies to victory that the best generals in France had taken only to defeat. It is believed that the founders of some of the great religions were so strongly believed in that they could restore the sick to health, the depressed to optimism, and the worthless to productive lives. Once the glory figure enters, all seems well.

Glory figures are able to establish, among others, some of the following ideas in the minds of their followers:

1. The speaker is not open to ordinary human frailities, but has more stamina, courage, insight, honesty, etc., than other people have—and more than most people could ever hope to have.
2. The speaker is one known as an individual of enormous power, whether it is power in speech, war, thought, politics, or the spiritual realm.
3. The speaker has expressed, without fear and with conviction, dedication to the movement represented by him or her in strong language and remarkable deeds.
4. The movement the speaker symbolizes is one that can be justified on the basis of social and cosmic sanctions. "The (Lord, people, times, world, etc.) is/are with us."

Indeed, humanity is sometimes lucky in having such glory figures. Churchill helped unite the free world, Roosevelt restored confidence in the nation—literally overnight—and religious leaders have focused the attention of people on the timeless problems that, when partly solved, create better people as well as a better world. In times of extreme crisis, such figures have helped humanity endure and triumph.

But we must remember that no one person is ever able to know all the goals a people should be seeking, and no one person is ever able to know and judge among all the ways of securing those goals. Such an enormous task requires a whole people to decide. Such a task can best be performed only by a democratic society of informed and intelligent people. But when we lack such a society, sometimes the unity and direction achieved by a glory figure can save a people from desolation and temporarily encourage growth.

But the glory figure is more often a fraud and a force for evil. Hitler and Stalin are modern glory figures who did their people great harm. These figures are often referred to as "fathers." Nevertheless, there are very good grounds for rejecting most glory figures most of the time.

> Of course, those who rejected paternalism were right to do so: paternalistic [glory figure] authorities hold out a false love to their subjects. False because the leader cares for these subjects only insofar as it serves his interests. . . .When Stalin declared "I am your father," he spoke a language which had no resemblance to exchanges between a real father and his children; there is no tolerance of their crankiness, no willingness to sacrifice himself—above all, no encouragement of their independence.[6]

Because the person posing as such a hero or heroine is frequently a fraud, this kind of ethos is not one that can be recommended. Moreover, it cannot be recommended to young people because, for them, it is a kind of ethos extremely difficult to develop; one runs the risk of appearing ridiculous. More importantly, it is an undesirable ethos for a democratic people. In a democratic state, or more accurately, in a state aspiring to become democratic, we—the people—should make the decisions; we should decide on the aims; and we should struggle with the problems of deciding on the means to achieve our aims. We must grow up, take responsibilities on ourselves, rather than

---

[6] Ibid., p. 82.

trust in someone to make decisions for us. We—society—must avoid situations in which only a glory figure can save us. Yet this pattern of ethos exists and is exploited. We should learn to recognize it, for more than one politician, general, or religious leader will try to capitalize on it. Unless we recognize "gloryism" we are apt to accept it and fall prey to it, rather than be able to help people recognize and avoid it. Although gloryism is a kind of ethos to recognize, it is not a kind we want, can, or usually need to develop.

Celebrity Figure Ethos

Another pattern of ethos comes from the need we all have to become the self we would like to be. Each of us has an image of what we want to be—the idealized image of ourselves. Because we need to achieve this image, but have not yet done so, we are more or less frustrated. If our idealized image is so beyond our present capacities—or in some cases, beyond any and all of our capabilities—the frustration may be very strong. The only way that the idealized image can then be "achieved" is by *vicariously* identifying with a person we perceive possessing the qualities of our idealized image.

Although Aristotle's analysis of ethos does not help us understand the ethos of the celebrity, recognizing that such ethos comes about as a means of gratifying an idealized image does help us understand the ethos of some people. Fans often live a drab existence as grocery clerks, mechanic's assistants, or kitchen helpers, and identification with the image of a rich, successful, popular, good-looking, and adventurous star offers vicarious fulfillment of a series of needs. William James suggested that the motivating power of an idealized image can be expressed as follows:

$$\text{The Strength of a Person's Idealized Image} = \frac{\text{Aspirations}^{[7]}}{\text{Achievements}}$$

Our self-image is the most frustrating when our aspirations and achievements are the most divergent. When we are frustrated

[7] *Psychology.* Vol. I. (New York: Holt, Rinehart and Winston, Inc.), 1890, p. 310.

the most, we are driven to identify with one who seems to have achieved what we would like to become.

The speaker who has developed celebrity figure ethos will establish some of the following ideas:

1. The speaker should be perceived as having come from a background similar to that of the audience: He or she should have been in the same plight, have had the same experiences, have come from the same socioeconomic situation, be helped by the same things, regard the same things as good and evil, have made the same mistakes, for example.

2. The speaker should possess characteristics similar to those the audience wants to possess but has not yet attained: to possess more daring, insight, charm, friends, cheer, skill, power, and wit, provided that the speaker can still meet the qualities described above.

3. The speaker should accept the members of the audience as the main core of humanity: as being of sound stock, as being the great majority or as being a member of the "forgotten" majority.

At first thought, celebrity figure ethos seems confined to movie stars and the like. But this is not the case. Many popular people are consciously or otherwise basking in the hopes of others. The popular student body president may have seemed to fulfill what other students would like to be. Some politicians have a similar appeal. Dwight Eisenhower was for many the fulfillment of an idealized image. He was a plain man, from humble beginnings, who rose through ethical means to the pinnacle of success. Photographs of the general entering Paris near the end of World War II show him standing on the runningboard of a Jeep, with a "typical American" grin, making the victory sign. He was the embodiment of the American success story. Many people in the United States identified with him and felt confidence in him because he had achieved what they would have liked to achieve. How different from the ethos of General MacArthur—a person who seemed to try to achieve glory figure ethos. MacArthur dismissed reporters who wrote about him as "Dougout Doug"—he was to be perceived as *General* MacArthur, with no nicknames, the man who knew what to do and how to do it. The old idea that politicians in the early days of the United States could succeed best if they could demonstrate that they were born in a log cabin and won fame fairly was based in part on the success of a person who has achieved what most people would like to achieve.

But the celebrity figure ethos is not a kind of ethos that we should base our hopes on. The painfully frustrated hopes of people caught in the dullness of life is a poor selector of who should lead and who should not: the need to enjoy the good things of life, to seek and find adventure, to possess vigor and good looks, and to excite admiration do not necessarily indicate who is best to lead. No one should look down on those who have not found better things to live for—and who among us would want less good looks, daring, skill, wit, wealth, and strength than we have? Nevertheless, when a person has achieved these things, it does not mean that he or she is also the wisest to select our goals and the means to achieve them. Generally such persons are superficial in their knowledge of goals and are unaware of the various means to achieve them; in fact, their success may be largely due not to wisdom but to luck. We should not capitalize on the frustrations of others by developing this kind of ethos, and we should be aware that it may select for us the most superficial kind of leader.

Agent Figure Ethos

A more worthy kind of ethos is found in the agent figure, which is the result of a still different need. Our society is specialized so that we no longer build our own house, educate our own children, grow our own food, arrange for our own protection, deliver our own mail, or build and maintain our own automobile. We elect representatives to achieve our political aims, hire teachers to educate our children, select a contractor to build our house, find a physician to care for our health, rely on a store to provide our food, and so forth. Consequently, there arises the need for experts, for agents who can achieve for us goals we have selected. These agents possess a special kind of ethos. We admire the sharp and proficient mechanic, the knowledgeable physician, the expert builder, and the gourmet cook. Because no one of us in our specialized society—and the same is true of "primative" societies, as well—can achieve all our goals, we award a kind of ethos to those who are expert at achieving these goals for us.

The speaker has Agent Figure ethos when the following ideas are suggested:

1. The speaker is dedicated to the achievement of a goal desired by the audience or that can be shown to be desirable.
2. The speaker is dedicated to the goal for its own sake or for the audience's sake rather than for personal gain.
3. The goal is practical but not merely crassly materialistic.
4. The speaker has caught the spirit and significance of the goal.
5. The speaker has a clear understanding of the barriers to the goal and the methods of reducing, eliminating, or circumventing those barriers.
6. The speaker's understanding is different from and better than that of others who also understand the problem.
7. The speaker's power, experience, ability, understanding, friends, etc., qualify him or her to secure the goal.
8. The speaker is a person who has helped the audience before, or people like those in the audience, or who could and would have had he or she been available.

Agent figure ethos does not offend the intellect as the other two patterns of ethos do. We need good agents—in politics, religion, and in life in general. Few can doubt in this day of our dependence on mechanics and other experts that we have too few good agents and that we ought to encourage more. When the need of an audience stems from specialization and all that specialization implies about the necessity of reliance on others, we can encourage others and become good agents ourselves.

The world of politics, however, is not the world of specialists, but of generalists. The politician and the citizen both vote on a wide array of programs requiring a knowledge of economics, medicine, ecology, energy, education, and military matters. A specialist cannot meet all the needs contemporary political life forces on one. More than just the expert, just the specialist is necessary. Therefore, agent figure ethos, although admirable in itself, is never enough. We should be willing to be good agents for those matters in which we are qualified, but the needs of our time require something more. Let us look at some of the possibilities before us.

Problem-Solving Ethos

The one great need of our times, although it is not always felt, is to develop and select leaders who can identify and solve a variety of our problems. Today human life is threatened by pollution of the air, land, and water; we face income-destroying inflation and, at the same time, rising unemployment; modern weapons can destroy all life by bombs, bacterial warfare, and chemical poisoning; millions of deserving people are held back from developing their full potential by systems of caste and prejudice. And yet, we know, some say, how to solve these problems.[8] We can create economic and political unions that would reduce, if not abolish, wars; we can produce enough goods to feed, house, and clothe our people, and, in fact, can produce so much that sometimes we produce more than can be bought. Yet the great problems of war, poverty, caste, tyranny, and, in most of the world, disease still plague us. It is clear that we need people who can help us solve these problems.

Problem-solving ethos is perhaps the ideal kind of ethos for those in politics. Interestingly enough, this kind of ethos follows

---

[8] For evidence that there are solutions to many of these problems, see Medard Gabel, *Ho-Ping: Food for Everyone* (New York: Anchor Books), 1979. If these solutions are adopted, the book holds, starvation can be ended by the year 2000.

Aristotle's analysis: The good problem solver is one who possesses intelligence, moral character, and goodwill. Let us list some of the kinds of ideas a person must establish to have good problem-solving ethos:

1. The speaker is a person of intelligence and practical wisdom, as shown by the following:
   a. A thorough knowledge of the problems we face because of his or her experience, study, and accumulated information.
   b. A clear mind free of unwarranted doubts or hesitations.
   c. Uncertainty about those matters in which uncertainty is warranted.
   d. Readiness to discuss the problems and their solutions.
   e. An understanding of the causes of these problems and of why they have not been solved.
   f. A perception of the importance of the problems and of the various solutions possible.
2. The speaker is a person of moral character, as shown by the following:
   a. Sincerity in the recommendations and viewpoints he or she presents.
   b. Faith in him- or herself as an agent of good.
   c. Dedication to the points of view he or she holds because these viewpoints are in the best interests of the audience and not for the speaker's own gain.
   d. Exemplification of the audience's conception of good moral character: self-reliance, desire for justice, optimism, kindness.
   e. Courage to stand by his or her views.
3. The speaker is a person of goodwill as shown by the following:
   a. Knowledge of the distinctive nature of the audience and sensitivity to its needs.
   b. Willingness to accept the judgments of the audience.

   c. Identification with the audience.

   d. Admiration of the good qualities and the acts and goals of the audience and willingness to overlook the shortcomings of the audience.

   e. Enjoyment in speaking to and being with the audience.

Not many people in politics exemplify these kinds of qualities, yet since these are the kinds of qualities we need, we should try to develop them in ourselves, and be able to spot them in others when they are present. If these kinds of qualities are needed today, those who have them should possess very persuasive ethos. These qualities, therefore, are worth developing.

Transforming Ethos

Men and women of great ethos—great teachers, great political and religious leaders—often have a unique ethos that, beyond merely solving problems, *helps people transform themselves into better people.* These people help us understand our potential and help us develop that potential. They understand the need for transformation and the possibility of it. They seem to be able to develop their own potential and to lead others to become like them. Thus, Socrates stimulated two thousand years of brilliant philosophy—for all philosophies in the Western world trace their ancestry to him. After Buddha, thousands of new "Buddhas" arise annually. After Galileo, a hundred thousand scientists come into being. Emerson said, "True genius"—and we must add, true ethos—"will not impoverish, but will liberate, and add new senses. If a wise man were to appear in our village, he would create, in those who converse with him, a new consciousness of wealth, by opening their eyes . . . ." After Thoreau and Gandhi, wave after wave of nonviolent protesters were born who set India free, who involved themselves in universal freedom for minorities, and who ended the Vietnam War. We might, with a slight paraphrase quote the first-century, A.D. rhetorician known as "Longinus": "Truly great ethos, when introduced at a seasonable moment has often carried all before it with the rapidity

of lightening." The person with transforming ethos, by a recon-
struction of personality, ensures that human beings rise. Although transforming ethos is rare, it is one of the great forces for
change. We must recognize this kind of ethos, and those who
can, must develop it.

Some of the following ideas are among the kinds that one with
transforming ethos will develop:

1. The speaker has a vision of what human beings and
   society can and should become.
2. The speaker has faith in him- or herself as an agent of
   desirable change.
3. The speaker's ideas would bring out the best in the
   audience and minimize and forgive the worst.
4. The speaker can release the latent powers of members
   of the audience and thereby give them significance.
5. The speaker excels in ways the audience wishes to
   emulate.
6. The speaker can unite members of the audience.
7. The speaker can find means by which members of the
   audience, if they commit themselves to his or her program for transformation, can become better human
   beings.

Although this kind of ethos is rare, if humanity needs it, we
must recognize its possibility, for some among us can develop it.
The rest of us ought to be able to recognize it so we do not
impede its development in others.

Achieving Ethos

What causes some people with ethos to have glory figure ethos,
and others to have agent ethos is still unknown. Probably luck,
interests, ability, and desires all play a part. Yet it is not impossible that, to a limited extent at least, we can choose a particular
kind of ethos for ourselves. We have a bit of historical evidence.
Benito Mussolini, Italy's dictator from 1922–1945 clearly had the
ethos of the "strong man." He appeared decisive, but actually his

ethos was a facade. Ethos can sometimes be "faked". But can we choose honestly to become someone who has and deserves to have a particular kind of ethos? Although the evidence is not very certain, it seems that, within limits, we can. If we wanted, for example, problem-solving ethos, we could begin by the study of problems, by travel such as would enable us to see such problems—and their solutions—firsthand, and by encouraging the friendship of those who helped us gain further insights into problems, their causes, and solutions. We would be building the foundations for being recognized as having a good problem-solving ethos. Just so, if we chose to have agent ethos, we could become an expert in a needed service—in medicine, repair, teaching, or the like—and spend time studying, experimenting, and working to develop our skills. Eventually, unless we were extremely unlucky, others who needed those skills would come to recognize our ability and would look upon us as an agent. Therefore, the possibilities for deciding on the kind of ethos we want to have are present. With a sense of modesty, and with a desirable degree of humility, we can and should chose a kind of ethos for ourselves. Moreover, the kind of ethos we decide on can be uniquely tailored for us. We can, with luck, become what we want to become, provided that what we want is not too far from possibility. The speaker should, therefore, decide on a kind of ethos for him- or herself and devise a program to achieve that kind of ethos in the shortest possible time through education, reading, travel, and whatever other activities may contribute to that end.

How the Speaker
Reveals Ethos

Reputation

To whom do delegates to a Republican or Democratic convention listen most carefully? When the candidate who is selected arrives on the floor of the convention, the candidate's reputation guarantees an attentive audience. Or if an ex-president speaks, the audience will listen. Ethos can come from reputation. But beginning speakers have no such reputation: and must establish ethos by other methods. Even speakers with a well-established reputation should not depend on their reputations as the only source of their ethos; they should attempt to develop it by the speech itself. Whether we desire it or not, our speech will reflect our ethos. Let us see how this is so.

Overt Choices

Just as the choices that we make in life tell much about the kind of person we are, so the conscious and unconscious choices a speaker makes tell an audience much about his or her nature. The fact that Lincoln, in his second inaugural address, chose to call for a peace "with malice toward none, with charity for all" suggests much about his ethos. The conclusion of this speech tells us that Lincoln was a humanitarian; it suggests his identification with the whole of his people; it tells us of a high moral purpose; it gives us a sketch of a plan that might have re-established the Union; it tells us of Lincoln's dislike for war; it perhaps suggests the only pattern by which peace can be made permanent. This choice by Lincoln gave him an ethos that will be cherished by people when his opponents' names are forgotten.

What someone chooses to tell us and how it is put suggests something about that person's attitude toward us, about his or her intelligence and moral purpose, and about the kind of person he or she is. The speaker who has chosen not to work very hard on a speech has told us something about him- or herself. The speaker who has chosen a subject of superficial nature has told us something about his or her quality of mind or about his or her energy. The person who chooses to wax pompously oratorical tells us something about his or her attitudes toward the audience and toward him- or herself. The speaker's choice of words tells us something about his or her background, intelligence, human sympathy or lack of it, and wit or lack of it.

The supporting materials you use suggest something about your understanding of people or lack of it, and your special experience with the problem, or your concern for the welfare of others. Your organization or lack of it may suggest a clear and able mind or a fuzzy and incoherent one.

Your sources tell the audience much about your background, education, and analytic ability or lack of it. Even your choice of words can convey to the audience that you are talking down to them, or that you are clear minded and well educated, or that you are a pompous exhibitionist. Your grammar may suggest that you are illiterate and your pronunciation may lend that idea further support. In your delivery, your approach to the platform, your freedom from notes, your ability to reflect a communicative attitude, your action or the lack of it, will say something, rightly or wrongly, about your nature. The tensions in your voice and skeletal muscles may suggest your emotional state. The number of small matters that reflect your ethos may well run into the hundreds. Virtually every idea you state, every bit of support you use, every word and gesture may say something about you. Thus it is inevitable that you build your ethos through choice of subject, choice of ideas, choice of supporting material, choice of words, choice of delivery methods, choice of organization, choices in methods of preparation, choices in the attitudes you express, and choices in methods of adapting to the audience.

Minimal Cues[9]

Frequently, the choices you make are easily noticed by the audience. If you become angry at a hostile question, for example, your anger is noted at once and the audience may infer that you feel insecure. Many choices however, have a more subtle effect on an audience. Some of your choices, mannerisms, and techniques are hardly noticed by an audience and yet exert a profound effect. The effects of these cues is most important in giving an audience an impression of your ethos. Consider the following case:

---

[9] Lew Sarett and William Trufaunt Foster, *Basic Principles of Speech*, Revised Edition (New York: Houghton Mifflin Co., 1946), p. 25. The significance of minimal cues was first suggested to this writer by his major professor of over forty years ago, the late Lew Sarett.

X was a woman of thirty-three. Her husband noticed that she had a habit of talking in her sleep. It occurred to him to turn the tendency into account. While she was talking in her sleep, he would say to her, in a very low tone, without waking her, "Tell me what you have been doing today, dearest." She would promptly comply. Soon she came to realize that her husband knew all her activities, even those she would rather have kept to herself and she came to the hospital to see if I could safeguard her against these involuntary indiscretions.[10]

This woman's husband may not have known it, but he was using one of the oldest techniques of persuasion. Why was it possible to circumvent her critical processes? It was possible not so much because she was asleep—that is only a superficial reason, but because *she was relatively unaware of the stimulus.* The husband succeeded in getting a response from his wife by establishing an idea without her awareness that it was being established. This stimulus was a *minimal cue.*

We can define minimal cue as any stimulus that is only dimly perceived by the audience. One psychologist explains cues in this way:

The response called "perceptual" depends, as we have seen, upon the presence of certain stimuli . . . It is important for us to bear in mind that frequently—if not as a rule—those *cues* or signs are *difficult* to identify. The perceiving person . . . is notoriously unable to tell in most cases just what it is that makes him [or her] recognize or estimate a situation as he [or she] does . . . .[11]

Frequently we establish certain ideas without the audience's awareness that they are being established. This necessity is particularly relevant to the establishment of our ethos. No speaker, for example, dares assert directly that he or she is intelligent. If a speaker announced that he or she is of good character the audience would either be suspicious or chalk the speaker up as self-centered and conceited. Nor can a speaker explain directly that he or she has good will toward the audience. We are sus-

---

[10] Pierre Janet, *Psychological Healing* (New York: Macmillan Publishing Co., Inc., 1925), pp. 212–213.

[11] John Frederick Dashiell, *Fundamentals of General Psychology* (New York: Houghton Mifflin Co., 1937), p. 458. This writer is also indebted to the analysis of Sarett and Foster, *ibid.*, Chap. 21.

picious of people who try to win our affection by direct means. *Yet intelligence, character, and good will must be established if our ethos as a speaker is to be a persuasive force.* At least, we do not trust people who are stupid, scheming, or who dislike us. The safest way to establish many ideas that contribute to our ethos is by using minimal cues.

Let us see how the process of using minimal cues to establish ideas works. Ordinarily we think that the more aware we are of a stimulus, the more compelling it becomes. Advertising slogans are repeated over and over in order to dominate our attention. If the fact that the traffic light has changed to green is not in the center of our attention, we don't react to it. What we are aware of is important, but stimuli *we are not aware of* also profoundly influences us. A group of psychologists at Cornell University were doing an experiment in which they were asked to look at a screen and imagine that they could see an orange. While they were looking at the screen, a picture of an orange was flashed on it, but with a light of such low intensity that no one could tell it was there. At times when the orange was not flashed on the screen the psychologists reported that it was much more difficult to imagine the orange and that it was much more difficult to "see"—yet they imagined a rather clear image of an orange whenever the invisible image was present.

As another example, the psychologist, Donald Laird, showed the effects of a minimal cue on the purchase of silk stockings.[12] He showed a large number of women four pairs of silk stockings that were identical except for one *irrelevant* stimulus: their odor. One pair had the usual odor characteristic of silk stockings: 8 percent believed that pair was the best in quality; 18 percent believed the pair with a sachet odor was the best; 24 percent selected the pair with a fruity odor; and 50 percent believed the pair with the odor of narcissus was best. The women did not notice the odors, even though the odor was the only difference in the four pairs of stockings and was a true minimal cue that influenced their behavior.

[12] Donald Laird, *What Makes People Buy* (New York: McGraw-Hill Book Company, 1935), p. 29.

Let us look at some other phenomena that are caused by minimal cues:

> The intelligent salesman perceives that it is time to close his interview. Something about the movements of the auditor's eyes, or . . . his way of sitting . . . in his chair, or his glancing at his papers . . . —something, though he cannot say just what it is, tells the salesman that it is time for him to go. Most of the so-called "sizing-up" of one man by another is a complex reaction to many obscure stimuli, which are not all catalogued or weighed but simply enter into the total mass of stimulation and help to determine the general impression. It is the operation of such minimal cues that often leads to the intuition or what is colloquially called the "hunch," and gives some basis to the claim that even a guess has a certain value.[13]

Minimal cues have much to do with legitimate (and illegitimate) medical practice. Believe it or not, the *color* of pills is important in medicine—sometimes more important than the chemical composition of the pills. Physicians have found that after a patient has responded successfully to a certain type of pill and the color is changed (but *not* the composition of the pill) from the original bright color (such as red or yellow) to blue, in an exceedingly high proportion of the cases, the patient will report that the blue pill didn't work. For some reason, coloring a drug blue makes it seem less effective. Certainly minimal cues also enter into the "bedside manner." The bearing of the doctor, his or her calm behavior, usually conservative dress, "little black bag", medicine, and Latin prescriptions are all devices that establish his or her prestige. A physician might make as fully competent a diagnosis dressed in long underwear, but it would never be accepted as competent. These small, irrelevant stimuli establish the idea that the doctor is a competent person whom we can trust.

Thus these minimal cues influence our ethos. It is virtually impossible to escape the tales minimal cues tell about us, because we are constantly exuding these small, fleeting stimuli. It is probably through such stimuli that a horse decides whether

[13] Dashiell, op. cit., p. 460.

its rider is experienced or a novice; through the rider's method of mounting, holding the reins, muscular coordination, and many other tiny stimuli the horse "knows" whether or not it may calmly trot back to the barn. Children are notorious for being able to size up a substitute teacher in a few minutes and to determine how much they can get away with; the ethos of the teacher creeps through and tells them something of his or her confidence and ability to command them. So it is with speakers. By the time a stranger has spoken for one minute, we already know much more about the speaker than he or she has told us. We have already formed an opinion of the kind of person he or she is, the attitude he or she has toward life, and his or her emotional state as he or she stands before the audience. So it is that a speaker gives an audience an impression of ethos by minimal cues as well as by reputation and overt choices.

Ethos and Ethics

We must ask now a question about the ethics of ethos: Can a speaker gain prestige by feigning a character that he or she does not have? Can a swindler appear to be honest? Can a person who despises an audience appear approving? Can a childish person appear mature? Can a shallow person seem deep? Possibly the number of times Brooklyn Bridge is sold each year would suggest that there is at least a modicum of truth in an affirmative answer to these questions; we have seen, for example, that Mussolini feigned ethos he did not have.

Yet the best way to appear to have good ethos is to *be* the kind of person who has had wide experience, who is of strong character, and who genuinely respects and likes people. Why is this? The reason lies in the manner in which an audience gets impressions of the speaker.

Recall the great number of cues you give an audience when you speak: virtually everything you choose to do—every muscular contraction, every variation in tone of voice, every word you utter, and every idea—can suggest something about your nature. If you believe you can control the long list of items presented, you are either more skillful than most or sadly misinformed. If you pose as the kind of person you are not, there will be a word, an accent, a misplaced idea, a self-centered notion that will escape you and arouse in your audience the suspicion that there is something about you that does not ring true. Nor does it take particularly keen intelligence or any arcane wisdom for the listener to sense a flaw. School children can sense the competence of their teacher, and a horse can tell whether the rider is in control or not. You do not have to be a genius to spot a "phony." The cues that give away the answer for better or worse are too numerous for most dissemblers to disguise or control.

Developing good ethos is a lifetime's work. It is not in the scheme of this book to explain how one should live to develop the qualities of ethos: insight, understanding, sympathy, and human feeling. Many students begin to stretch their horizon while studying speech; they begin to develop moral fiber and to catch a glimmer of the worth of other human beings. The difficulty is not that we cannot develop such qualities, but that too few of us ever try.

Exercises

1. Among people you have known personally, select two with very good ethos and two with very bad ethos. What kinds of qualities resulted in each? Could each, in your opinion, have developed better or worse ethos? Explain your answers.

2. Among political candidates, who, do you think has strong and desirable ethos? Can you account for the ethos of that candidate? Does the candidate do things—send out minimal cues or display choices—that interfere with his or her ethos? Explain.

3. Study the life of some historical character who has been noted for powerful ethos. How was this ethos developed? What matters impeded the development of the person's ethos? Could other characters living at the same time have had the same quality and strength of ethos? Explain.

4. Which of the kinds of ethos mentioned in the text seem most suitable to you? Which kinds would you least like to have? Justify your choice. Will the kind of ethos that you have ten or twenty years from now be different from that kind you might want now? Explain.

5. Explain how you could develop problem-solving ethos. Set out a program to increase your knowledge about the major problems besetting people and the causes of and solutions to those problems. How could you develop compassion for those who suffer?

9
Delivery*

Developing Confidence

The dread of most beginning speakers is the lack of confidence popularly called "stage fright." It is the most universally reported problem by beginners. No list of the effects of stage fright need be presented; anyone who has experienced it knows them well enough, and the symptoms differ from person to person. But those who experience stage fright can be assured that, except in extremely rare cases, it can be partly controlled. Moreover, when properly controlled, stage fright furnishes energy the speaker would not otherwise possess and can stimulate and quicken thought so that many speakers think better in front of an audience than in the less stimulating quarters of their room. Let us look at the sources of controlling this problem and of developing confidence to replace it.

---

* Although this chapter is last, some instructors may want to assign it earlier, depending on the course procedure.

Some Reassurances

Should you suffer from stage fright, it may surprise you to know that most likely, no one, including the instructor, will know it. Audiences have been found—as have speech teachers—to be quite unable to tell if the average speaker has fear or confidence. Listeners will, as surveys have shown, greatly underrate the degree of the speaker's turmoil. So if you do have some qualms in front of your class, *act as if you didn't*, and no one will know your feelings.

It may help you, also, if you realize that your stage-fright—which is by no means limited to the stage, but is found in any anxiety-producing situation—is experienced by more than ninety per cent of your classmates. Your instructor realizes you may feel discomfort; your classmates will be pulling for you; no one will or should pay much attention to any overt signs of the problem; when everyone is a beginner, mistakes are not just tolerated, but expected. Moreover, if you work to control the problem, you may very soon be at a comparative advantage with your class.

Finally, know that the problems of discomfort in front of an audience tend to reduce markedly with experience, especially with experience in front of the same audience. After you have spoken to your class a few times, you will most likely note an encouraging decrease in discomfort and the beginnings of confidence. And it might help to know that as you grow older, the problem will become less severe, even if you do nothing actively to resolve the problem.

The Nature of Confidence

You can understand how to increase your confidence best when you realize the sources of confidence. Let us take some examples. If you have ice-skated, boxed, skied, or learned some other "risky" sport, you probably lacked confidence at first and experienced the same kinds of symptoms novice speakers sometimes do. But as you learned the skill, your early almost incapacitating fears left, and as you developed mastery, your confidence rose, and may have risen so much that you became overconfident and made mistakes. *Confidence is built by knowing what to do.* When you first drove a car you were, and should have been, worried, anxious, and nervous. But as you practiced the skills of driving, your fear disappeared, and disappeared far more than the dangers of driving warrant. If you were afraid of fighting, and learned some techniques of fighting, your beginner's fears disappeared; confidence—courage—often comes from *competence.* If a normal person is unduly afraid of something, you can teach that person competent ways of behaving in the situation, and the fear will disappear. Because competence is built from simply knowing what to do, you will be learning what to do in this speech course. You have a good speech, and you *know* it when you choose a significant topic, outline it clearly so that the audience can follow it easily, and support it with materials that are sure to hold the audience's interest, that validly demonstrate the logical merit of your case, and that involve and motivate the audience. You will not feel that you will disgrace yourself; your own competence will make you *want* to speak, and it will, as in any sport, help you do so with confidence. Therefore, to develop confidence, always pay close attention to the skills that will help bring your competence to its highest peak. Be sure you understand the assignment for the speech, and bring to the assignment all the competence you have. If you have not worked to develop competence, if you have chosen a subject you think is not very significant or interesting, if you have not worked to choose strategy with care and shrewdness, if your supporting material is commonplace and boring, and if you have not built your ethos and given thought to how to involve the audience, you either are apathetic to your fate—which some students are—or will find yourself in for an agonizing case of stage fright. But it need not be so; remember: *Wherever fear strikes, if competence can be developed, fear can be reduced.*

A second source of confidence is harder for most people to develop because Western culture has not emphasised it: *Commitment to a cause as a source of confidence.* Martyrs have

burned at the stake without a whimper; protesters have im-
molated themselves without fear. Now if strong commitment
can eliminate any sign of fear in those who end their lives to
further a cause to which they are committed, it might do more
than a little to lessen the weak-in-the-knees feeling on the occasion of a practice speech in an elementary speech course. Intense commitment can lead to confidence and even to courage.

You may already be committed to one or more causes so
strongly that you have been driven to speak when others might
have been fearful. (Commitment may also drive you to increase
your competence, thus greatly increasing your courage.) But not
all college students have developed strong and intelligent commitments. How do people locate those principles, causes, and
ideals, worth their dedication?

Sometimes college is a good place to find causes that can take
us out of ourselves, that can enlarge our life, that can give us a
sense of greater worth. The study of history—if your instructor or
your reading are good enough—can shine light on worthy commitments from the past that can serve the future; literature is
often about the nature of one or more kinds of commitment and
the results of such commitment; ethics is the study of different
commitments and of different ways of evaluating commitments;
anthropology and sociology can help us understand the commitments of different peoples the world over; religion, science,
philosophy, and the arts all can give powerful testimony to
commitments that have driven people wisely and foolishly. Nor
does being in college guarantee finding ideas and causes to
support; in fact, often commitment will not be the main concern
of college courses; you may have to look in your own libraries,
selecting materials carefully and reading imaginatively. Or, you
may find a source of commitment from observing life itself. The
problems of this age, and the opportunity we have for solving
them are greater than the spirit of the age suggests. We know
how to—for the first time in the world's history—produce enough
to feed, house and clothe everyone on earth. There is, at this
moment, enough food for all—provided we take our calories, in
the form of grains, vegetables, and fruits and not in the form of

meat. The enormous progress of science and technology, however, has not been met by equal progress in solving the social problems that have eroded other cultures. Life offers much that is worth commitment.

When we find matters worthy of commitment, often we *becomes* committed. But sometimes we find matters worthy of commitment, but do not become committed. What then? All of the great religions have developed exercises to help keep commitment high. We might study the techniques used in Buddhism, Judaism, or Christianity and apply them to secular matters. That these religions are thousands of years old is testimony to the certainty that they have ways of developing and keeping commitment among their initiates. We have much to learn about developing commitment as a source of courage and confidence. We do know this much: Strong commitment can reduce pain, anxiety, and fear; it can increase strength and ability and can stimulate superior speaking.

Developing confidence is, therefore, the development of knowing what to do. Developing *competence* is developing a belief so intense that it destroys self-consciousness and obliterates a sense of danger. Either confidence or commitment can greatly reduce anxiety and increase confidence; together —although in our culture they are a rare combination —they can help develop an explosive release of ability that increases ethos in ways that can captivate audiences. Besides reducing stage fright, competence and commitment are worth having for their own sakes.[1]

Delivery

Poor delivery can ruin the greatest masterpiece of discourse, as those of us who have sat through bad acting in great plays can testify. Good delivery can greatly increase the peak of attention

[1] For a more complete discussion of the development of confidence, see my chapter in Otis M. Walter and Robert L. Scott, *Thinking and Speaking: A Guide to Intelligent Oral Communication*, 4th ed. (New York: Macmillan Publishing Co., Inc. 1979), Chap. 7.

paid by the audience. A well-delivered speech should hold a much higher peak of attention than the same speech read individually by each member of the audience. The very best delivery can even get and hold attention from an audience when the material is dull, at least for a brief time.

Delivery, although important, is the least intellectually challenging of the subjects of rhetoric, and a greater bulk of nonsense has been written about it than on any other aspect of rhetoric. There are, nevertheless, procedures that will help a speaker quickly develop the ability to use delivery well.

The Nature of Good Delivery

Good delivery makes the meaning and spirit the speaker intends to express as intense as possible. Each idea, each sentence, each image, each word should be delivered so that with appropriate intensity interpretation is as easy as possible for the audience. The function of good delivery, therefore, is to wring from the speech all the power possible.

Good delivery, as well as intensifying a speech, should suit the speaker. Delivery that "suits" you is not necessarily the kind that is "natural" to you. You may unconsciously mumble so that the audience can't understand the speech or jingle the coins in your pocket or the necklace around your neck. These habits not only distract the audience, but suggest that you are nervous, uncommitted, or distracted. What is natural to you may not be what is best for you as a speaker. Yet, your delivery must not be so foreign to you that you are forced into long, tedious, and unnecessary practice sessions to develop an alien skill that some may perceive as a false front. It is doubtful that a voice teacher could have improved the eloquence of Franklin Roosevelt or Winston Churchill. Delivery, without distracting you from your ideas, must spring from your own nature.

Your delivery must likewise contribute to your ethos. (See Chapter 8.) There are stories about actors who could bring their audiences to either tears or laughter by reciting the alphabet. Although you may never develop—or need—such ability, you cannot escape radiating hundreds of minimal cues in delivery that will say something about your sense of competence and commitment, your attitude toward yourself, your feelings about the subject on which you speak, your attitude toward the audience, and your general estimate of your speech. The way you walk to the platform, the way you look over the members of the audience before beginning while waiting for their attention, the way use or misuse notes, your smile—or lack of one—the tension in your face and arms, your use of bodily action, and the sound of your voice all send messages about you, rightly or wrongly, to the audience. Minimal cues in delivery probably do more to establish or destroy ethos in beginning speakers than any other single device.[2]

Developing Good Delivery

Early in this century, and especially in the nineteenth century, delivery was taught by assiduous and boring attention to its "atoms." Certain people, "elocutionists," had analyzed what they believed were the elements that made up voice, posture, gestures, and facial expressions. Elocutionists were following an idea that had, in the natural sciences, produced many significant breakthroughs; they thought that the same idea, applied to speech delivery, would yield equal results. But ideas that work in one discipline may not in another, and elocution, although filled with hundreds and hundreds of elements in pitch, use of time, volume, and the like, simply became a vast complex of knowledge that was useless. Few people can control hundreds of elements at one time. Elocution, moreover, resulted in the artificiality for which it is still known and condemned. There was something wrong with the idea that every person must use every element in exactly the same way. Elocution died, but not until nearly every practicing elocutionist had died, too.

[2] One reason to not assign this chapter until after at least the first speech is that when speakers realize how delivery radiates minimal cues, that knowledge may make them more apprehensive in front of an audience. The chapter should be read when the instructor senses the students are ready for it.

Delivery is not a matter of complex elements. Good delivery can be characterized by just one quality: a full understanding of the importance of your words as you speak them.[3] Let's put it in another way: you must run the ideas through your head before you run them over your vocal chords. Or: good delivery shows that you grasp the meaning and significance of each word or group of words and their relation to each other and do so *vividly*. Perhaps the best way to put this Gestalt approach to delivery is that *you must respond to what you say as you are saying it.*

A few cautions must be noted. Of course to have a vivid understanding of an idea as you utter it does not mean each word and phrase must sound as important as if it betokened the crack of doom; to understand what you say as you say it means that less important words, phrases, sentences, and paragraphs will receive less note. Nor can such delivery as we hope for come when you are so fearful that you cannot really respond to your ideas; confidence must come first. In fact, good delivery so powerfully forces your attention on your own ideas that it helps, slightly, to reduce self-consciousness. When your attention is on the idea you want the audience to comprehend, it cannot be on self; hence, you cannot be self-conscious but will be idea-conscious. Finally, it is possible to develop such a delivery quickly; long and arduous practice sessions are not necessary because good delivery is forming the habit of paying extremely close attention to what you say, and responding to what you say rather than the fearful plight of being before an audience.

This quality of good delivery is easily demonstrated. Say a few sentences to a friend and have the friend say a few to you. Write down what each of you has said and then each read your own part aloud. If the first conversational encounter was real conversation, it will have the lively sense of re-creating thought at the moment of speech; the read version of the conversation will

[3] This approach to delivery was first discovered by Richard Whately, in 1828, *Elements of Rhetoric*, Douglas Ehninger, ed. (Carbondale, Il., University of Southern Illinois Press, 1963), Part IV. The approach was later expanded by James Albert Winans, *Public Speaking*. (New York: Appleton-Century-Crofts, 1917). See especially p. 31. Winans's followers continued to nonatomistic approach developed here.

lack that very sparkle. Your instructor can demonstrate the difference between the two qualities, or you can do it yourself: Take any passage with which you are familiar and read it aloud without thinking about it more than is necessary to recall the words. Then read it several times more, asking yourself, each time: Am I reproducing the thought, the image, the idea, the feeling *before* I say it? Feel it first and then say it. After a bit of practice, you will be able to re-create the thought powerfully as you speak. When this habit is formed it will not be easily lost. You will be able to deliver speeches very well without arduous practice and eventually without any practice.

Suggestions for Practicing Delivery

At first the skill of delivery may come slowly. The following suggestions will help you speed the development of good delivery:

1. Prepare the speech thoroughly so that you know you have a good product; this knowledge will help you avoid feelings of dread or failure.

2. Make a clear, careful outline of the speech and learn the outline by heart. To learn a one- or two-page outline—if it is well constructed—takes the average college student about seven or eight minutes. Learn the outline so well that you can repeat each item from the bottom to the top. An outline so well learned will not be forgotten; you will not have to fear forgetting the major ideas of your speech.

3. Practice the speech from the memorized image of the outline, *working hard to re-create the meaning and feeling of each word and each idea.* When you have an image ("The only window in the room was broken and stuffed with newspaper to fill the broken part, while the rest of the window faced a dank, decaying brick wall an arm's reach away") you must take the *time* and *effort* to re-create in your mind's eye each image before or as you tell of it.

If you develop this kind of delivery, you will have your very own style, one suited to you alone. Moreover, you will be able to make important ideas and words seem important to the audience, although you may do it in a way different from that of another person using the same words. You will have the variety in voice that helps hold the audience's attention, and that variety will help you reinforce the meaning of what you say. You will not develop a monotonous repetition of sound patterns—sometimes called ministerial melody—that makes your ideas less powerful and less fresh. Finally, you will be able to wring from your material all the strength your ideas and words deserve, and perhaps more. At any rate, you will be a more thoughtful, interesting, and effective speaker.

10

Assignments in Exposition and Persuasion

ONE OF THE best ways to learn the techniques of exposition and persuasion is to give speeches, to evaluate speeches, and to be evaluated. Therefore, thirty assignments are given here—many times more than can be performed in a semester. These assignments, moreover, lend themselves to many useful and interesting variations, which should make it possible for the instructor to meet his or her aims and the needs and abilities of the class.

The speaking assignments begin with the easiest and progressively become more difficult. The first speeches begin with explicit standards to help guide the student; but as the assignments become more varied and complicated, standards are no longer given with the assignment in the hope that the student will set the standards.

These assignments will help focus the work in class and provide interesting and challenging activities that will lead to the development of intelligence in informative and persuasive speaking.

The Exposition of a Statistic

Introduction

Although figures lie, and liars figure, accurate statistics are often indispensable in a good expository or persuasive speech. Some statistics are either too large or too small to be understood; others are so dull they require some sharpening techniques to make them interesting. This assignment will help you learn to use a statistic so that it will be clear, interesting, and effective.

Assignment

Deliver a one- to two-minute speech in which you select a statistic that needs sharpening and use *at least* two ways of sharpening it. You may, for example, show us how great 93,000,000 miles is by (1) telling us how many generations it would take to walk that far, (2) telling us how many freight carloads of shoes we would have to take along (experts say a pair of shoes is usually good for 1,500 miles of average walking). Often a barrage of as many as ten methods is more effective than only a few.

Be sure to choose an absolute figure for your statistic: an amount too large to be understood easily. Do not use ratios, fractions, or percentages; they are already clear, and sharpening techniques are unnecessary and unworkable.

Techniques for Sharpening Statistics

Use any of the following techniques that will make your statistic clear and vivid to the audience:

1. Break it into comprehensible units.
2. Compare it with other items.
3. Use charts and diagrams.

Subjects

The cost of the last war; the amount of soil eroded each year; the cost of a commercial airplane or ship; the size of the solar system, of the Great Galaxy, of interstellar space, or the number of stars or galaxies in space; the wealth of the United States, its income, its productive capacity in industry and agriculture; the population explosion; the amount of money spent on research, charity, or education; the private, state or national debt; the national income or gross national product; the distribution of income, of savings, of liquid assets, or of property; federal expenditures on foreign aid, social welfare, interest on the national debt, "pork barrel," agriculture, defense; the amount of money spent on tobacco, alcohol, gambling; the cost of unemployment, strikes, crime, accidents, illness; the number of cells, neurons, blood vessels in the body; the power of the nuclear bombs; the age of the earth; the size of the sun; the amount of water, sand, oil or coal known to be available.

Standards

In evaluating your speech and those of your classmates, consider the following points:

1. Was the speaker's statistic (and his or her computation) accurate? Do not, be too specific. Instead of saying "$287,974,965.53," it is clearer and still accurate to say "almost $290 million."
2. Did the speaker give the source of the statistic briefly but clearly? Remember that in some digests of statistics, such as encyclopedias, almanacs, and statistical abstracts, the source for each statistic is not the publication itself, but the one given (usually in very fine print) at the bottom or top of the statistical chart. Both sources can be unobtrusively mentioned.
3. Did the speaker use a variety of devices to sharpen the statistic? One device may make clear, but a *barrage* of devices for sharpening the figure may make the figure so impressive that the audience will remember it and be influenced by it.
4. Were the methods used to sharpen the statistic vivid, clear, and accurate?
5. Did the speech fall within the time limits?

Making a Point by Examples

Introduction

A speaker who covers too many points in a speech is like a hunter who goes big-game hunting with a shotgun. A shotgun will make many little "hits" in the side of an elephant, but it cannot bring down a charging bull. The more sagacious hunter will use a rifle, which delivers the total power of the shell behind only one bullet; the bullet, if rightly aimed, will kill, but the scattered shot cannot.

The most common fault among beginning speakers is that they do not know how to use a rifle. They make many points poorly instead of limiting themselves to one carefully selected but crucial point. As such, beginning speakers do not "kill" but only irritate.

A speaker must limit the speech to a few carefully selected points and establish each one thoroughly. In this assignment, bring down an audience with one carefully selected and thoroughly supported point.

Assignment

Select an important idea; state the idea in a single sentence; and support the idea for three to four minutes with examples that make the idea vivid and compelling.

Techniques for Using Examples

I. Have only one point or generalization and no unnecessary subpoints that are also generalizations. The following outline has unnecessary subpoints:

A. Some teachers must work weekends and vacations in order to make expenses.

(1). This time should be spent in continuing the teacher's education.

a. A teacher I knew had to work each night in a bar.

b. Another teacher ran a farm to supplement his income.

      c. A good teacher left the profession because
      he could not properly provide for his family
      on a teacher's income.
(Clearly, 1 is an unnecessary generalization. Omit such sub-points.)

2. Make the illustrations vivid by the techniques of imagery, narration, and characterization whenever possible.
3. Do not use atypical illustrations. Show that the real illustrations are typical by using statistics or a barrage of
   instances.
4. Use hypothetical examples if such examples add vividness and clarity to the speech.

Subjects

Avoid trite, overworked, superficial subjects or such trivial or
obvious ones as "baton twirling is fun," or "falling snow in the
winter is a problem for northern cities." Although a creative
person might make these subjects more satirical and more
pointed than they appear to the prosaic mind, most speakers
would probably spend time more effectively on subjects of more
significance. In any event, avoid prosaic treatments of such
subjects.

Some subjects will need to be limited so that they become
one-point ideas and are directly supportable by examples without the intervention of additional general statements. The following are some suggestions for appropriate subjects:

A characteristic of creativity or of genius; a cause of the
down-fall of civilization; a cause of personal success or of
failure; a needed reform in our schools, prisons, mental hospitals, local or national government, courts, unions; a necessary
change in foreign policy, business practices, divorce laws,
religious institutions, civilizations and subcultures, treatment of
ex-felons or of the physically handicapped, treatment of racial or
cultural subgroups; a necessary change in our attack on the
problems of crime, corruption, mental health, ignorance,
poverty, disease, inflation, water polution, tyranny, energy

shortage, productive capacity, election or appointment of officials.

Civilizations fall because of . . . (failure in problem solving, moral corruption, poverty, war, and so on); great art is that which . . . (creates a single emotion, causes empathy, has a unity of form, or attempts to communicate an idea that cannot yet be put in words); great literature . . . (is written in response to the times in which the author lived, is always "avant garde," or has any other characteristic you believe to be significant.)

Use examples to demonstrate that any popular theory or any of the above theories of history, art, literature, and the like are false.

Standards

1. Subject: Was the general statement the speaker chose of sufficient significance to merit taking the speaker's time and the time of the audience?
2. Opening: Did the speaker avoid opening with apologies, irrelevant ideas, or general statements? Did the speaker, instead, open immediately with one or more of the best examples?
3. Strategy:
   a. Was the general statement phrased in its clearest and most vivid form?
   b. Was this general statement repeated frequently enough so that it was clear to the audience?
4. Tactics:
   a. Did the speaker use the techniques of making the examples vivid: fresh and powerful imagery, narration, and characterization?
   b. Did the speaker's examples have enough logical merit to build a substantial case for the general statement?
5. Did the speaker conclude the speech with a note of finality? One should conclude either with the strongest example or with a strong restatement of the point.

Using Analogies

Introduction
One function of the analogy is to present the experience of similar groups. For example, when we want to know whether a certain idea might be good for us, it helps to know whether it was good for others.

Assignment
Deliver a three- to four-minute speech in which you urge us to accept a certain idea by showing that it has been true or has worked for similar groups. Be sure to use at least two analogies.

Techniques for Using Analogies
Logic demands that you demonstrate two matters for each analogy.

1. The point you advocate *must have been true* in the past. For example, if you want to argue that we should adopt the honor system, you must show that it has been successful at other universities. If you want to show that cultures decline when human values are neglected, you must show that other cultures *did decline* when these values were overlooked.
2. We are in all significant respects *similar* to the groups in the examples. (Note the exception discussed in the text.)

Subjects
Probably the easiest way to meet the assignment is to select an idea or plan that would be desirable for your class, university, city, county, state, region, or country and to show that a similar idea has worked under similar conditions. You can as easily show that an idea or plan would fail because it has failed for others in similar situations, or that an idea that has worked for others would *not* work for us because the situations are different.

Standards

1. Did the speaker introduce the point with a well-dramatized statistic or vivid illustration, description, or narration?
2. Did the speaker state the point clearly? (While stating the point, watch the audience carefully to see whether they understand it, and if they do not, make some adjustment tto make sure they do grasp it.)
3. Did the speaker show that each analogy met the two logical requirements described under "Techniques of Using Analogies"? (A minimum of *two* comparisons must be used.)
4. Did the speaker summarize the idea carefully (but not mechanically) after each comparison?
5. Was the subject chosen worth the time of the class?
6. Was the conclusion of the speech strong and clear?

Using Testimony

Introduction

Fraudulent use of testimony can be found in advertising and propaganda. Examining breakfast-cereal testimonials and cigarette ads will produce examples. Testimony, of course, can be used well; it is, moreover, indispensable because whenever you give statistics, illustrations, and ideas *that are not directly experienced or gathered by you*, you are using the testimony of someone else. Care should be taken to see that testimony is well chosen and well used.

Assignment

Select a point that can be supported by the testimony of authorities, and prepare a three- to four-minute speech in which you demonstrate your ability to support a point by using testimony. Use the testimony of at least *two* authorities. These authorities may be

1. An individual, such as an expert who has made a special study of your topic.
2. A group who make up a fact-finding commission, a board of inquiry, or an investigating committee.
3. An authoritative publication such as *Who's Who* or *The Statistical Abstract of the United States.*

Generally, you will find that the testimony of your authorities is abstract; you will have difficulty, therefore, in keeping the class interested in your point. The best way to keep them interested is to introduce your point with a description, an example, or dramatized statistics vivid enough to capture and hold attention.

Technique for Using Testimony

The most difficult problem in using testimony usually is to show the audience that the agent giving the testimony is a genuine authority. For each authority you quote, you must take special care to demonstrate that he or she is an authority:

1. Show that, by virtue of experience or study, the authority is in a position to know the specific facts and problems involved in the matter on which you are quoting him or her. The mere mention of a title often is not enough. If you can, name the experiences the authority has had that have earned him or her the right to speak, and quote some well-known colleagues who testify to his or her reputation.
2. If the authority may be open to bias (such as a politician testifying about his or her own works or a scientist hired by a corporation testifying about the product of the corporation) the authority must be cleared of bias if the testimony is to be accepted. If, of course, the authority is not in a field in which bias is important, you need only show that he or she is qualified.

Subjects

It is not necessary to use a list of subjects because almost any complex subject leads itself to the assignment. Most of the subjects from previous assignments will lend themselves to this one.

Standards

1. Did the speaker select one point for the speech? The speaker must be sure that all the authorities selected support the one point. Each bit of testimony will, of course, be a subpoint, but it should be a *relevant* subpoint.
2. Did the speaker introduce the point by a vivid description, dramatized statistic, illustration, or narration? Sometimes two or three of the above forms make a better introduction than only one.
3. Did the speaker support the point by the testimony of at least two authorities?
4. Did the speaker take special care to show that each of the authorities was qualified in the area for which he or she was quoted? If necessary, was he or she shown to be free of bias?
5. Did the speaker use repetition and restatement effectively? The speaker should watch the audience carefully as he or she states the point to be sure they understand it.
6. Did the speaker conclude the speech with a note of finality?
7. Was the subject worth the time of the audience?

Using Concrete Forms of Support

Introduction

This speech represents a variation of the previous assignments. Instead of limiting support to only one form of support, support your point with any or all kinds of support. Review the previous assignments for instruction.

Assignment

Select a point and devise a three- to four-minute speech in which you support this point with statistics, examples, analogies, testimony, visual aids, or some combination of these.

Technique for Using Concrete Forms of Support

1. Use *only* one point *without* subpoints. It is difficult to remain with one point for a number of minutes because you must have discovered many descriptions, anecdotes, and instances to support the idea. Good support is not easily found.
2. The forms of support used should make the point vivid.
3. In addition to being vivid, however, try to achieve strong logical validity with at least some of your supporting material, so that the speech is more than merely interesting.

Subjects

Whatever subject you choose, be certain that it lends itself to support by concrete forms. Generally speaking, limit yourself to a small aspect of a larger problem. Instead of speaking on the subject "We should have socialized medicine," break the subject into smaller parts and choose only one. The following are acceptable examples: "Many Americans are not receiving good medical care"; "Too many communities do not have the proper medical facilities."

The farmer (laborer, teacher, lawyer, student) needs a break; "Genius is 90 per cent perspiration and 10 per cent inspiration;" you ought to see Mexico (our national parks, Canada, Europe, the art museum); Why the civilization of Greece (Rome, Egypt, China, Maya) fell; A great person is one who lives for others; You ought to study psychology (philosophy, history, science, art); Our divorce (labor, tax, civil rights) laws ought to be revised; The Democratic (Republican) party has given us our greatest statesmen; Physical handicaps can produce a great soul; Our schools (prisons, mental hospitals, city government, teachers, churches, business groups, federal government, courts, state legislatures) are not fulfilling their function properly; Great art universally has a unity of form (a single emotion, a way of making one feel empathy); or any other subject that lends itself to the assignment.

Standards

1. Was the point selected of enough significance to merit the time spent on it?
2. Did the introduction open with one or more of the following concrete forms: a striking statistic, a vivid illustration, or a strong comparison?
3. Were the number of general statements severely limited so that each could be supported in such a way as to make it interesting and valid?
4. Did the speaker demonstrate the accuracy of the data and the accuracy of the inferences well enough to raise a strong logical presumption for his or her general statements?
5. Were the general statements carefully supported with concrete material that was interesting: real illustrations, hypothetical illustrations, dramatized statistics, comparisons, testimony, and so on? (Visual aids should be used wherever they will add interest and clarity.)
6. Did the speaker use some of the following devices competently to achieve clarity: forecast, final summary, repetition and restatement, evidential summary, cumulative summary?

Expository Speech Assignment

Introduction

There is probably more expository speaking done today than there is speaking of other kinds. Yet we rarely hear a *good* expository speech—one that is clear and at the same time interesting. The techniques of developing clarity and interest, however, are relatively simple. Moreover, these techniques are a prerequisite to the use of more difficult techniques.

Assignment

Prepare an eight- to ten-minute expository speech designed to instruct and inform an audience.

Subjects

Art: Explain any theory of art, such as the theory of significant form, Plato's theory of art, the nature or significance of any painter or period of painting, the nature of modern art, and so on.

Anthropology: Explain the customs, institutions, attitudes, or significance of any other culture or of any subculture in our own society.

Astronomy: Explain any theory of the origin of the universe or explain the nature of a galaxy or describe any planet or star or the like.

Biology: Explain any principle of cell life, the phylogeny of any part of the body, the function of any part of the body, or the like.

Economics: Explain any theory of economics, such as the theory of price determination or the law of diminishing returns.

Geology: Explain any natural phenomena, such as glaciers, cold fronts, oil deposits, and so on.

History: Explain the causes behind any fact of history; or the effect on history of any force, such as geography, climate, or economics; or the significance of any period in history.

Literature: Explain any period of literature, the characteristics of any great writer, why any play or novel is important, or some other aspect of literature.

Religion: Make clear the nature of any religion (except your own) or explain the significance of religion in history.

Mathematics: Explain the nature of algebra, geometry, the calculus, or some other area of mathematics

Music: Explain any theory of music, make clear the contribution of any great composer, explain the history of any musical form such as the symphony or the opera, describe the nature of modern music, or the like.

Physics: Explain any principle of physics, such as Newton's laws of motion or Einstein's theory of relativity.

Philosophy: Explain any particular school of philosophy, such as logical positivism, stoicism, phenomenology, idealism, or any system of esthetics, ethics, logic, metaphysics, or the like.

Political Science: Explain any principle or problem of government, international relations, or the like.

Psychology: Explain any significant principle of psychology, such as a principle of learning, adjustment, or perception.

Sociology: Explain any significant principle of contemporary sociology, any school of sociology, or some other aspect of sociology.

Standards

1. Was the subject chosen an important and significant one?
2. Did the speaker show that understanding of the subject?
3. Did the speaker limit the number of general statements to a minimum and state each clearly and vividly?
4. Were all general statements carefully selected so as to be absolutely required by the speech? Were they crucial? Were they "patterned" so that they had a clear relation to each other?
5. Did the supporting material make the general statements clear and vivid?
6. Was the conclusion of the speech clear and strong?

Magazine Assignment

Introduction

A good speaker can interest an audience in ideas and motivate it to act. One method of achieving interest and motivation and one of the most basic methods of persuasion is to create or encourage a *wish* and then to show that certain courses of action can gratify the wish. Using this technique, you are asked to create an interest in one of the magazines listed here.

Assignment

Give a six- to ten-minute speech in which you interest the people in your audience in a magazine so that they will remember its basic nature and may one day read it with some regularity.

Techniques for the Assignment

1. *The "wish technique":* Begin by arousing curiosity or a desire for the kind of material contained in the magazine. Encourage the desire for the information by pointing out its importance and utility. After you have aroused the desire, show how the magazine can help fulfill it. The wish technique must be carefully executed so as to include the maximum of specific facts, comparisons, information, illustrations, and statistics; if it is executed only with general statements, it will not be successful.

2. *Clarifying the nature of a magazine:* Most of your time should be spent making the nature of the magazine clear and interesting. The nature of the magazine must be set forth in concrete form. Instead of telling the audience that the magazine has articles on economics, tell about some of the important and interesting material you have found about economics. It will be helpful to compare or contrast the magazine with other similar magazines.

Magazines

The following periodicals are worth examining:

American Heritage	*Fortune*
American Scholar	*Harper's Magazine*
Atlantic	*The Nation*

Changing Times	*The Nation's Business*
Congressional Digest	*New Republic*
Consumer Reports	*The Reporter*
Current History	*Saturday Review*
Daedalus	*Science Digest*
Fact	*Science News Letter*
Facts on File	*Scientific American*
Omni	*The Skeptical Inquirer*

A Critical Review

Using the "Magazine Assignment" as a guide, prepare a critique of any of the following newspapers and magazines, pointing out its strengths and weaknesses:

Your home-town newspaper	*Newsweek*
The New York Times (Especially the Sunday edition)	*Reader's Digest*
	Saturday Evening Post
	Ladies' Home Journal
The Christian Science Monitor	*Esquire*
	Catholic Digest
The Louis Post Dispatch	*Christian Century*
The Wall Street Journal	*Atlantic*
The Washington Post	*National Geographic*
The National Inquirer	*Life*
The National Observer	*U.S. News and World Report*
Time	

All of the preceding magazines have had highly critical articles written about them. Be sure to consult a recent *Reader's Guide* about your magazine or about, for example, the type of magazine you have; for example, look under "News Magazines."

Persuasive Speech Assignment

Introduction

Because persuasive speaking can steer and energize whole civilizations, persuasion must be used intelligently, and when possible, brilliantly. A society without persuasive speakers must either be directed by force or be inert and apathetic. Therefore, intelligent speakers should understand and use the techniques of persuasion.

Assignment

Give an eight- to ten-minute speech in which you select an important idea for which you want to secure acceptance. If time permits, plan for a question period following your speech.

Techniques for Speaking Persuasively

1. *Rhetorical logic:* Because rhetorical logic requires the use of evidence, be certain that you have supported your ideas with vivid and valid statistics, examples, analogies, and testimony.

2. *Emotion and motivation:* Be sure to select your main points so that they are few in number and of such a nature that they can arouse an emotion and motivate an audience.

3. *Ethos and the speaker:* By choice of ideas, supporting material, and delivery, try to suggest to the audience that you are a person of clear-headed intelligence, of good character, and that you have goodwill toward the audience.

Ten Variations of the Persuasive Speech Assignment

1. Select an idea to which you think the audience is hostile and construct an introduction that will build your ethos

and, thus, open the minds of the audience to you as a person. Then transfer the audience's acceptance of you to your ideas and proceed with the speech.

2. Persuade the audience to accept (or reject) a piece of legislation currently before the state legislature or the Congress.
3. Persuade the audience to accept (or reject) a viewpoint that answers the question, "What sort of life should one live?"
4. Select an idea that your audience already favors and, by using the strongest psychological techniques, increase its acceptance of the idea.
5. Give a speech in which you try to persuade your audience to act as a group in the performance of some worthy endeavor in your community.
6. Give a persuasive speech designed to create goodwill for an organization that deserves goodwill.
7. Give a speech persuading the audience to reject an organization that perhaps now enjoys, but does not deserve, goodwill.
8. Give a speech persuading the audience to admire a person because of his or her ethos, because of his or her accomplishments, dedication, contributions to humanity, and the like.
9. Give a speech persuading an audience to reject a person because of his or her selfishness, duplicity, lack of intellectual leadership, or the like.
10. Persuade an audience to accept the one idea that you believe is the most important idea in the world today or to reject the one you believe is most dangerous.